MEXICO
A NEW SPAIN WITH OLD FRIENDS

MEXICO

A NEW SPAIN WITH OLD FRIENDS

by

J. B. TREND

.

CAMBRIDGE

AT THE UNIVERSITY PRESS

1940

CAMBRIDGE
UNIVERSITY PRESS

University Printing House, Cambridge CB2 8BS, United Kingdom

Cambridge University Press is part of the University of Cambridge.

It furthers the University's mission by disseminating knowledge in the pursuit of education, learning and research at the highest international levels of excellence.

www.cambridge.org
Information on this title: www.cambridge.org/9781107502055

© Cambridge University Press 1940

First published 1940
First paperback edition 2015

A catalogue record for this publication is available from the British Library

ISBN 978-1-107-50205-5 Paperback

For

CARLETON, ELIZABETH AND DAMARIS

in New York

CONTENTS

ILLUSTRATIONS

Chapter I

INTRODUCTION

Modern Mexico has been described in all its aspects. The work has been done partly in Mexico, partly in England, but mainly in the United States; and the best informed American writers have shown that rare sympathy with Mexican things which only comes with real understanding of Mexican aspirations.

I cannot hope or attempt to do better what has already been done in America. I could not, if I tried; while my ever-increasing admiration for the United States, and the innumerable friendly people who live there, would prevent me from intruding on what, after all, is more their concern than mine. Mexico may have been "the New Spain", *la Nueva España*; but its people are not now Europeans but Americans; whilst I feel myself to be incurably European, and my only qualifications for writing about the New Spain are that I have had more experience than most people of the old one, and can overhear most things that are said in most kinds of Spanish. I have known Spain intimately for twenty years, and have been fortunate enough to make a large number of Spanish friends; and when I think of Spain—of the Spain I knew—of what it has been and what it may be again, the words "Spain" and "Spanish" clearly mean a great deal more to me than they do to most modern writers on Mexico, who have never been in Spain in their lives.

To me, of course, there is "another Spain", just as (in 1919) we became aware that there was "another France" which was not exactly that of M. Clemenceau; and—as I try to suggest sometimes to those who raise their eyebrows at the rulers of modern England—there is still "another England": a country which once produced statesmen and administrators, and still produces writers and men of science; a country, above all, of poets—of Promethean poets, to borrow the phrase of a Spanish poet now resident in Mexico—including not only Shakespeare and Keats, but Langland and Milton, Shelley, Byron and Swinburne; men who not only wrote poetry, but who protested in poetry, as well. When I am alone in another country, avoiding English people and English news-papers, enjoying the society of other friends and the intel-lectual exercise of speaking, thinking and writing in another language, it is the poets whom I most like to think of as English; the poets, and then the eccentric, quixotic English-men, the "mad" Englishmen, the type which everyone in other countries has known or heard of, and which may be, after all, the only type of Englishman which anybody in another country can really admire.

It was the "other Spain" which first took me to Mexico. During my long visits to Spain in the early 'twenties, when I discovered that procrastinating in a country was the best way of cementing friendships, I met one or two Mexicans and found them eminently likeable. On my last visit to Spain in 1937, in time of war and invasion, I met other Mexicans and liked them no less than the countrymen of theirs I had met before.

Now Mexicans, as one would naturally expect from their history and temperament, have a clearer vision of recent events in Spain than most other Spanish Americans. Charitable and quixotic citizens of Mexico (like charitable and quixotic people in England, the United States and several other countries) had found homes for some hundreds of homeless Spanish children; and just as my own remote, fenland seminary had looked after some thirty Basque children with a few academic Spanish people and their families, giving them the means of going on with their work which the war in Spain had interrupted, so a few Mexicans had got together and arranged for some Spanish scholars to come and live in Mexico, and go on with their work under the protection of Mexican hospitality. It was done rather quietly; to do it otherwise would have made things uncomfortable for all concerned. But it was done more thoroughly than had been possible in England or anywhere else. The invitations were issued to men whom the Mexican authorities definitely wished to invite, on account of the particular kind of work they were doing or because of their intellectual distinction. They were to live, according to the old formula of Mexican courtesy, *como en su casa*, as if they were in their own home. They were no longer invited guests, strangers, but old inhabitants, *pobladores*, who were now coming back, like all good Spaniards, to the oldest and most familiar of their homes, to that which their great-great-great-grandfathers had made the living image of Spain.

By this thoughtful and generous action of a few public-spirited Mexicans, the idea of "the New Spain", *la Nueva España*, has recovered its old meaning and gained a new one. It was a noble gesture, and one which showed a magnificent spirit: this invitation by a "Spanish House" to a number of the best representatives of that Spain which can never be destroyed, the Spain which is a country of the mind; and it is a lesson which Spaniards—all good Spaniards—will take to heart. Spain is not done for; she will go on and begin again in Spanish America. Spain has been called the mother of beginnings.

So the Mexican *Casa de España* will one day come to be regarded as nothing less than another beginning, a new birth. As with the University in Exile, in New York, a new cultural relationship has been established between the Old World and the New. Like New York, Mexico has set a fine and stimulating example. Mexico has not been alone, either, in its far-sighted plan of assistance to Spanish intellectual exiles. Chile, too, was determined to see what could be done to help; it sent its best poet to Europe on a "crusade of salvation", and his activities have already borne fruit. Colombia and other South American republics have generously received Spanish exiles of character and intellect; while Cuba formed a Committee of Assistance, a *Comité de Ayuda a los Intelectuales Expatriados*, to save Spanish culture. From all corners of the continent men came forward to do what was possible to tide the Spanish people over this difficult and disastrous moment of their history. Mexico and Chile had shown the way, and many other Spanish-American countries began to follow them. At this time (December 1938) the war in Spain was not yet over; but it was clear that, in most countries, the cultured and civilized people were uncompromisingly on the side of the Republic.

The project for the foundation of the *Casa de España* in Mexico had found a warm supporter in President Cárdenas. For Mexico, Spaniards are the most desirable of all immigrants, racially and historically the most closely identified with the Mexican people; and the country has need of such valuable and useful settlers, who come there with no idea of getting rich quick, like so many of their predecessors, but with the hope of living peaceably in a free country and being as useful citizens as they can.

In the case of intellectuals, and others who arrived when the war was over, the Mexican authorities took special care to select the immigrants personally: medical men and men of science, scholars and writers well known in their particular fields, skilled workers and specialists likely to be valuable in the industrial development of the country, agricultural labourers from the arid and sterile uplands of Spain, who would bring their experience and their endurance to the more varied climatic conditions of Mexico. Among the original members of the *Casa de España* were some of my oldest Spanish friends. They included one scholar who had previously been living as a University teacher in Cambridge. It was clear, therefore, that the time had come for me to go to Mexico as well.

Through the "New Spain" (or the "Other Spain") I have been able to get into touch with the "New" (or "Other") Mexico. This is not the Mexico of scare headlines, violent abuse, or the patronizing, philistine attitude of certain European writers. It is not the Mexico of those who come to make propaganda about oil or keep alive the fiction of religious persecution.

My Mexico is not like that; nor is it the Mexico of archaeologists, of students of Indian "folk-ways", or even of the pressing social problems with which modern America is beset. All these have interested me; but they have been adequately studied, and in most cases admirably studied, in the United States.

My Mexico (if I may call it that) is the Mexico of reasonable Mexican people—of those who, without prejudice, are really and honestly trying to make Mexico a better country for Mexicans to live in; such, for instance, as President Cárdenas, and the parents of my small friend Emma. For Emma is the Mexican Alice in Wonderland, who will one day go through the looking-glass and become the most important person in Mexico—a Mexican citizen.

Chapter II

TRAVELLING TO MEXICO

Going to Mexico, I found, made me go to school again, to the first school I could remember; and even that, when I thought of it, turned out to be no use. What geography did we do there? I have no recollection whatever. Later on, a preparatory school left somewhat clearer memories of France and South America; but I never remember doing Mexico or Spain or even the United States, though that preparatory school was the best school I ever attended. Like many people, I suppose, I have learned my geography by actually travelling over the countries concerned, in Europe, North Africa and North America; just as I have learned my modern history mainly from the introductions to Baedeker's *Guides*. Mexico presented a geographical problem which had to be taken more seriously.

To begin with: how was I to get there? Was I to go by sea, and enter Mexico at Veracruz, or go overland from New York? Time was short. On my first visit, all I had was a Christmas vacation which, however, was allowed to begin rather early, in the first week of December. I chose the overland route from New York, by St Louis, to San Antonio, Texas; and from there I flew to Brownsville, on the Mexican border, Tampico and Mexico City. The second time I went by sea, from New York to Veracruz.

The first twenty-four hours from New York got me as far as St Louis, where I changed trains. It was dark when we left, and our crossing of the Mississippi and the long journey along the farther bank made no impression. It was different on the way back; ascending the great river on a bright, frosty morning on the last day of the old year, and finding it full of ice. Yet the second morning after leaving New York I was in Texas—"Yes, *sir*: I've been in Texas", said the man in the serial story, tapping his hip-pocket—But all that was years ago. The Texas that I awoke to began with miles upon miles of oil-wells, each with its peculiar, diagrammatic Eiffel Tower; while now and again a well would be alight, sending up an enormous, slowly flickering column of dark, heavy flame. Conrad Aiken has described the whole journey in a memorable fashion in *A Heart for the Gods of Mexico*. Did I, too, see a negro porter, carefully putting his peaked, railway-man's cap into a paper bag as the train left the station? No, that was afterwards, in Mexico; and instead of a paper bag, the cap went into a black cotton one. Was it Little Rock that offered the vision of a colossal Capitol, as large as the one at Washington, and as white and shining as the one at Havana? I remember the building, but have forgotten whether the place was called Little Rock.

I stayed the night at San Antonio, Texas. "You stop at the Blue Bonnet," a friend had said. Imagine a hotel called the Blue Bonnet at San Antonio, Texas! I imagined it: a small pleasant hostelry, with suggestions of the Wild West and the Deep South, in a quaint Spanish-American, or American-Spanish town, surrounding the old Spanish fort of the "Alamo". But San Antonio, Texas, is like a Swedish town in semi-tropics, a large and attractive modern city, well planned and well built, with over 230,000 inhabitants and spread over a very considerable area, with the central blocks carefully arranged to make the most of a narrow, canalized, winding river. While as to the Blue Bonnet hotel (named after the lupin which is the State flower of Texas), it has between seven and ten floors and is one of the most up-to-date hotels—as well as one of the most friendly and comfortable—that I have ever stayed in, anywhere. No less than three taps to the basin in your private bathroom: hot, cold and—iced! I should hardly have been surprised if it had been eau-de-cologne, whisky, or some even holier spirit. An excellent dinner in what was called a coffee-shop; while afterwards, in the Lounge (or whatever it is called in Texas) I was accosted by one friendly soul after another, trying to say nice things about England, condoling with its difficulties, hoping that in the end it would be "O.K.", and then excusing themselves by saying that they were of pure English extraction. The interest in England and the sympathy for individual English people—though not necessarily for the Government—was vivid and striking from the moment I landed in New York. English writers and English reviewers are apt to assume that the average American can know no more about Europe than the average Englishman knows about America. Nothing is farther from the truth. In America there is no unofficial censorship, as there was, even in peace-time, in England; the press can print as much of the news as it likes, with the result that a New York taxi-driver may know more about European affairs than many members of London clubs or college combination-rooms.

Next morning I had to be up before sunrise to catch the aeroplane for Brownsville. I left the charming Blue Bonnet soon after six and had coffee in a little stall across the street. The plane was half an hour late at the airport, and one of the air staff invited me to more coffee, with the delightful manners of a hospitable undergraduate. When the plane arrived, it was full of sleeping individuals, reclining in chairs tilted back as if they were at the dentist's. Lights were screened; but the passengers had mostly covered their faces with hats or newspapers. There was, however, a hostess. She won my heart by bringing still more hot coffee, and an excellent map; while presently, after we had been in the air for some minutes, she came back with a card, giving the height, temperature, barometer, force and direction of the wind; and at the bottom, "Hostess: Miss Martinez."

At Brownsville (Tex.), on the Mexican border, there was a

change of plane and an inspection of papers. Mine were in order; but a special letter to the "Agent of Migration", saying that I was "a good friend of Mexico and Spain", certainly made things easier; in fact, the Agent of Migration waved me through.

The first stop in Mexico was Tampico. (Memories of M. W.-J. and an oil company in 1914! Tampico was, through him, the first place in Mexico which ever seemed real to me, and I still have a map he sent me pinned up inside a cupboard at home. M. W.-J. knew enough Spanish to realize that the peons had a case; and as he was, in a small way, a landlord himself at home, he may have thought the titles of an oil company in Mexico rather dubious. On one occasion he rationed the revolutionary forces with bully beef: "...how rebel chieftains Shared your beef-tins...." Our letters sometimes dropped into verse, and our verse generally ended in a competition of Thackerayan or super-Thackerayan rhymes. We last saw each other at Roulers, in Belgium, in October 1914, before the Germans blew it to pieces. "What shall it be?" "Clar't", said M. W.-J., who knew his Jorrocks. And clar't it was.)

The plane from Brownsville to Tampico had followed the coast, and seemed to steer by the long, sandy bar or reef, which divides the blue water of the Gulf of Mexico from the turbid water of the lagoon. Travelling in Mexico makes one want to rub up not only the remains of school geography, but also the notions of elementary botany. Geography and botany are the principal keys to what one is seeing. There are history and archaeology, of course: but the history is in many of the books (especially in modern American books) while the archaeology, once studied by an older generation of Englishmen (Maudslay, Joyce, and Thomas Gann) has now become an American subject too (and with "American" I here include Mexican archaeologists as well). Botanical information is not so easy to come by. Yet the things which grow in Mexico are among the objects which most strike a traveller from Europe.

You do not have to go far to look for them; they are always before your eyes.

Now England is not exactly a country devoid of growing things. Even in midwinter, a well-run garden will always have flowers growing outside, in the open air, or at least trees and shrubs with bright red leaves or berries or curiously shaped hanging fruits which show up against a pale grey sky. England, and especially the flatter parts of England (like Cambridge), is a country which makes those who live in it notice little things. People who occasionally take me for country walks seem intensely aware of all sorts of processes going on and things growing up, in every hedge and bush and tree; while a Spanish undergraduate was fascinated by the typical landscape of Cambridge, "because you can see the shapes of the trees against the sky".

But in England, unlike Mexico, we have seasons very clearly marked off from one another: while in England again (and even in Scotland and Wales) there are only a few hundred feet between the highest level at which things grow, and the lowest. In Mexico, on the other hand, you can never be quite sure what time of year it is; while the supremely important thing is not, "Are you in the North or the South?" but how far are you above the level of the sea. You can, at any rate, by merely looking round, be pretty sure whether you are down in the tropics not far from the sea, or half-way up in the comfortably warm temperate zone, or on the high plateau near Mexico City. You can not only feel the temperature, you can see by the plants.

ΖΗΣΟΝ ΩΣ ΕΝ ΟΡΕΙ

(Live—or, perhaps, boil—as on a mountain.)

That is a quotation from Marcus Aurelius, which a former headmaster of mine had inscribed in letters of gold over his fireplace. I asked him once why he had it there; for, as an irreverent schoolboy with a taste for science as well as for languages, I could not believe that his little brass kettle would boil at a lower temperature for being 600 ft. up, which was the altitude of the particular mountain on which my school was situated. "Well," he answered, "in the early days, h'm, then in the middle days, and now in the latter days, h'm, I have always lived upon an hill, h'm...." This was somewhat exceptional, perhaps, even if the hills were only little ones; but my h'm-inspired headmaster was an exceptional and remarkable man.

In Mexico, living as on a mountain is exactly what you have to do, because in fact you are always living on one, except when entering or leaving the country by the ports of Veracruz or Acapulco, or visiting the Maya temples of Yucatán or the tropical forests of Chiapas. At these places you can do all the things which you would not do on a mountain: leave off all the garments which the police will allow, or sit out of doors until the small hours with your coat off. Marcus Aurelius ought to have said—perhaps he did say, somewhere—that one should not live carelessly, as at sea-level.

On the coasts of Mexico the temperature remains practically the same all the year round, and there is no great difference between the temperatures of day and night. The drop in temperature (as I found afterwards at Veracruz) comes when the north wind begins to blow.

Things change when one begins to climb up to Mexico City.

Chapter III

ARRIVAL

No sensible traveller nowadays would pretend that you see nothing from an aeroplane. In fact, in travelling by air along the coast of Mexico from Brownsville to Tampico (as in flying down the coast of Spain and over the delta of the Ebro) I saw things which I might never have thought of, as far as Mexico was concerned.

First, there is a belt of coast of variable width, formed of sand, partly flat, and partly in dunes heaped up by the wind. This is the "sea-marge sterile". There are no trees; the wind is too violent for that; and in the Gulf of Mexico it blows hard for six months, from October to March. But the sand-banks, even though they have no trees, have a dense, greyish growth of plants, said to be grasses, milk weeds, buck-wheat, convolvulus, and so on. Inside the sand-banks are grasslands interrupted by lagoons of still, stagnant water. From the aeroplane, they showed with peculiar colours: crude yellows and greens like the oxides of certain metals produced in elementary chemical experiments; I could almost distinguish the masses of scum floating on the surface. Actually the lagoons are the breeding place of millions of malarial mosquitoes.

The airport at Tampico is behind the town, and between two of these lagoons. It felt decently and heavily warm—for December. There were tropical flowers; to have a garden, or at any rate flower beds, is thought necessary to the civilized aspect of a Mexican airport as a garden is to an English country railway station. In Mexico I cannot remember having

seen many railway stations with gardens; though Acámbaro
(where you leave the main line to go to Pátzcuaro) and
Uruápan (where that line ends) have not only gardens in the
stations but groves of trees as well—eucalyptus and cedars.
The Tampico airport not only had flower beds, but tiny blue
flowers growing everywhere on the short, closely cropped
grass. The town of Tampico looked tidy and well ordered—
from the air: a different place, probably, from what it was in
M. W.-J.'s time, in 1914.

The plane went inland, but mainly southwards, and rose
to 12,000 ft., right above the clouds; though that was not for
the first time. It had been above the clouds after leaving
Brownsville; above a floor of clouds. After an hour or so,
mountainous country became visible between breaks in the
cloud beneath us; then the conical top of Popocatépetl. We
were nearly there. Then the outskirts of Mexico City itself,
looking like toy farms, with their low buildings surrounding
wide courtyards. Iztaccíhuatl, the other mountain (the
"sleeping woman"), beside her companion, Popo. At the
airport, a collection of old Spanish friends and a new Mexican
one. Among the few other passengers in the plane—she had
posed rather adroitly for a photograph at Tampico—was a
friendly, charming, sensible American woman, who spent
most of the time writing letters and postcards in a large,
round hand. We presented our papers to the "Agent of
Migration" side by side, and I discovered that she was Mary
Pickford.

That afternoon in Mexico was memorable. We got in a
good deal, without any sense of hustle. A lunch at a medical
club in which I was gently introduced to some of the less
peppery Mexican dishes. An exhibition of paintings by a
Spanish friend, showing that exile had not soured him, while
his own particular problems of form and light, arrangement
and colour, still interested him—if anything more deeply than
before. It is a serious thing, to find oneself, in middle age—

he was fifty-two—an exile in a new and strange country, with none of one's books or pictures, and all one's possessions in a single suitcase; and it is a possibility which English people, too, will have to consider; for, owing to circumstances beyond a private person's control, the same thing may happen to us.

Spanish people, of course, are not altogether strangers in Mexico, nor is Mexico altogether a strange country to them. There is the great bond of the language, and the fact that, whatever the anthropologists may say, Mexico is, in many ways, extraordinarily Spanish. Instead of gypsies there are Indians; that is the chief difference, and I am not sure that Mexico has not the advantage. The difficulty has been that, since Mexico became independent, the Spaniards who came to the country were sometimes of the wrong type. Their ideal (though it was not always realized) was to get rich quick and eventually go back to Spain, which meant that the Spanish immigrant might be anything from a company promoter to a barber or the proprietor of a night club, but had no genuine or lasting or intellectual interest in his adopted country. Further, these *gachupines* always tended to favour reaction; they were supporters of General Franco, and the General himself has been described by Mexicans as the *fuhrercito gachupín*. Now for the first time Spaniards are being invited to Mexico, not as business-men *gachupines*, but as intellectuals. Many of them were old friends; and among them the painter of the pictures we were looking at.

He had changed his style in some ways since he was in Madrid. He would put on the canvas one thing, one object suggested by the mood of the moment. That object needed another object to balance it, and so the composition grew. The results were Hieronymus Bosch-like fantasies: a hill with windows, a tree with bare branches suggesting a miniature tree on which to hang jewellery—the sort of thing I used to see on my mother's dressing table—while in the distance was a woman with her back turned to another little tree, and putting the jewels on. Another picture showed a woman's head, a

shadow, and behind her an Indian. There were two versions of
this, and several good portraits. The painter, at any rate, was
working and not despairing of his exile. He had also written
his first impressions of Mexico, which would certainly interest other travellers; they have been reprinted as *Cornucopia
de México*, by J. Moreno Villa (Mexico, 1940).

We next drove through the woods of Chapultepec to the
Desierto de los Leones—an ancient monastery, but no more
a desert than its inhabitants were monastic, to judge from a
seventeenth-century English monk, Thomas Gage, who made
fun of the Mexican friars, though as a good Catholic himself
—his apostasy did not take place until twenty years later—
he had no motive for his malice except Catholic truth. Like
many of the resorts of monks and holy hermits the place is
charming: high up in the hills to the south-west of Mexico
City, and shrouded by high trees—a forest reserve, in fact.
"Resorts", says Terry's *Guide*, the only modern guide-book
which approaches the style and spirit of Richard Ford's
inimitable *Guide to Travellers in Spain*, "resorts which though
referred to as deserts and jejune places, often were flower-
crowned retreats where milk and honey and frankincense and
myrrh took the place of the Barmecide repasts supposed to
be their daily refection."

Nearly 10,000 ft. above the sea, the Desierto is a thickly
wooded estate, with deep gullies and running water all the
year round. The trees are mostly evergreens, pines and oaks;
but it is also—like Uruápan—a place of ferns and mosses.
The woods round the monastery and all the country leading
up to it were densely green, even at this time of year, in the
dry season. The monastery garden was laid out in 1606, but
a few scattered rose bushes are all that are left of it. Mrs Hulse
Matschat, author of an interesting book on *Mexican Plants
for American Gardens*, thinks that the ancestors of these roses
must have been brought from Spain. I have an uncertain
recollection of tall salvias, crimson and blue, blooming in
December in the Desierto as they do at that time on the

mountain-passes leading to Puebla and Cuernavaca, though I cannot swear to them; but I particularly remember a bluish red-hot poker, or something very like one. Later in the year, in July and August, there were masses of wild flowers, mints, umbelliferae, and composites, in these deep, moist woods; while in May the most striking things are the high flowering shrubs, especially the arbutus trees, with their masses of delicate, white blossoms. In fact, for many people, the Desierto de los Leones would be an earthly paradise.

It was beginning to get chilly, though not yet dark, when we left the Desierto and went back to Mexico by the Obregón Monument at San Angel. President Obregón, the man who ended the civil war and promptly sent out missions to teach the Indians to read and write, was having lunch at a restaurant, when he was shot by a Catholic caricaturist—a man who made funny drawings for a clerical newspaper. The country was horrified. Obregón, besides being a great public benefactor, was a genial, friendly soul whom people really regretted. The restaurant was bought, and its grounds turned into a garden, while a striking sculptured monument was erected, with powerful and beautiful figures in four groups, one on each side of the monument. In front is a rectangular tank, and steps (in the manner of a pre-Spanish Mexican pyramid) leading up to a room in the monument, or rather a gallery from which you look down on to a piece of the original pavement where he fell, and read his last words: "I have faith...in the Revolution." There is said to be a bloodstain, but I did not see it. Far too many visitors to Mexico see bloodstains and persecution everywhere, forgetting that there have also been bloodstains and persecutions in their own countries, and not least in Europe. We should not forget the famous French chateau which the guide treats entirely as a background for the murder of the Duc de Guise.

It had been a cloudlessly clear afternoon, and we had had many glimpses of the two volcanoes, Popocatépetl and Iztaccíhuatl, glistening all snowy against an intense blue sky.

Mexico, from Chapultepec

Mexico: Monument to Obregón

(And this, as I had to keep reminding myself, was the month of December!) The volcanoes are generally called *Popo* and *Izta*, for short; but I discovered how they were pronounced, and found with amusement that they both went—in accent and intonation—to a well-known opera tune, perhaps the best-known tune in the whole range of opera: *La donn' è mobile*. So instead of "poppa-catta-petal" you say *pópocatépetl*, and for "Izta", *ista-síwatl*, and sing them to the tune of mi : mi : mi | sol., fa : re : - | - : re : re | fa., mi : do.

By this time it was decidedly cold, and I remembered that we were not in the tropics after all, but on the top of a mountain—strictly speaking, a valley 7000 ft. above the sea with a very different climate from that of Tampico or San Antonio, Texas.

Mexico possesses three different climates, according to the height above sea-level. Modern geographers give more: the latest geography of Mexico distinguishes ten, which it numbers from A to J. But the three main climatic divisions, depending on altitude, correspond also to zones of vegetation and agriculture; you can not only feel that you are in a certain climate, you can see it around you. The three regions are:

(1) *Tierra caliente* (hot land), from sea-level up to about 2600 ft.

(2) *Tierra templada* (warm land), from 2600 ft. up to about 6000 ft.

(3) *Tierra fría* (cold land), above 6000 ft.

Hot Land includes the coastal belt, as I saw it first from the plane between Brownsville and Tampico, or from the train coming up from Veracruz, either through that decorative, but drizzly town, Jalapa (4491 ft.) on the narrow-gauge railway, or through Córdoba (2712 ft.), Fortín (3330 ft.) and Orizaba (4005 ft.) on the British-built Mexican Railway. It includes the dry peninsulas of Yucatán and Lower California, godless Tabasco, the Isthmus of Tehuantepec with the tropical forests of the State of Chiapas and the borders of

Guatemala, and also hot Pacific ports like Acapulco. The hot dry region to the south of the Central Plateau is also sometimes counted as Hot Land, especially the mountainous region between Tehuacán and Oaxaca which produces such strange and peculiar cactuses.

Warm Land includes Cuernavaca (5072 ft.) and Taxco, where careworn administrators and foreign ambassadors (to say nothing of innumerable tourists) go to recover from "altitude"—from not obeying the precept of Marcus Aurelius. Warm land, that is to say, includes the moist valleys at the edges of the central tableland, especially that place of paradisal subtropical gardens, Uruápan (5313 ft.) on the Pacific slope, as well as dry and extra dry areas like the high plains stretching northwards from Querétaro (5983 ft.), San Luís Potosí (6138 ft.); and, farther to the west, Guadalajara (5082 ft.) and the Lake of Chapala which D. H. Lawrence described in *The Plumed Serpent*, and, in the south, Oaxaca (5000 ft.) where he wrote *Mornings in Mexico*.

All, or nearly all, the other places in Mexico that anyone is likely to have been to or heard of, are counted as Cold Land, and lie well beyond 6000 ft. above the level of the sea: Mexico City (7392 ft.), Puebla (7031 ft.), Toluca (8712 ft.), Guanajuato (6623 ft.), Morelia (6223 ft.) and the lake district of Pátzcuaro (6742 ft.).

Mexico, then, is not really a tropical country, though more than half of it lies within the tropics. It has three distinct climates, according to the height above sea-level: *caliente*, *templado* and *frío*; hot, temperate and cool. It is not the latitude which determines the temperature, nor is it the time of year; the average temperature at most places is pretty much the same all the year round, but what that temperature will be depends mainly upon the height above the sea. The three divisions give a general idea not only of the average temperature, but also of the look of the country and the vegetation, and what everyone will experience in travelling quickly up to Mexico City or going quickly down to the coast. An altitude of 7000 ft. means a considerable reduction of air-pressure and more particularly of oxygen; and these facts show themselves in human beings by a slight deafness on arrival—a deafness which unfortunately does not lessen the din of superfluous motor horns or badly tuned loudspeakers; or a feeling of breathlessness after even mild exertion—one is warned never to run upstairs or run after trams or buses; or sometimes, again, altitude makes itself felt in frantic and constantly recurring neuralgia.

If these are effects of altitude from which plants are happily immune, there are others which affect plants no less than men. In the middle of the day there is always a certain amount of warmth; but about sundown comes a sudden and considerable drop in the temperature. This daily variation is greater than anything I ever experienced in the south of Europe, especially during December and the first two months of the year, when the thermometer may fall as much as 50° F. in about an hour. In the rainy season too (July, August and part of September), the daily downpour brings about a considerable cooling of the air; in fact, the climate of Mexico City during those months seemed to me to bring autumn mornings, summer middays, and spring evenings. This daily variation in temperature is, of course, an event of the greatest importance in the life of Mexican man as well as in the distribution of Mexican plants. What its effects are on the Mexican character and temperament, I should hardly like to say; but it is obvious that such sudden changes will prevent many tropical trees and flowers from growing on the high plateau of Mexico City; for though they receive a sufficient amount of heat by day, they are exposed after sunset to low temperatures which they cannot stand.

Still, the fact remains that the amount of heat received by living things in Mexico is very considerable, even in the cooler months; at certain hours of the day the seasons can hardly be distinguished from one another, and the difference only becomes apparent later in the afternoon. Actually January is said to be the coldest month; but even in January one can become very hot in the sun, for the dryness of the atmosphere allows the rays of the sun to pass through it without loss of power. It is this dryness of the atmosphere which is characteristic of the climate of the greater part of Mexico. For, with the exception of the coasts (and not even all of those) and part of the slopes of the Sierra Madre (the mountain range running down the middle), the air of the rest of the country seems to have hardly enough moisture to support the vegetation it does. The vegetation of Mexico, even of the high plateau of Mexico City, is endlessly varied; nothing in Mexico struck me so much as the things seen growing there. Yet the plants of the dry, cool country are not to be compared with those of the hot, damp climates at a lower altitude, where there is regular and sufficient rain.

A member of the Botany School at Cambridge, when I tried to express my difficulties and state my contradictions, was at once able to explain the principles of the change. The kind of vegetation, he said, in the tropical zones as in the temperate ones, is determined by four things: heat, rain, winds and soil. The main thing is heat; the type of flora, in so far as it depends on existing conditions, is dependent primarily on that. But the finer differences in the vegetation within a climatic district are chiefly determined by the soil, and then by the amount and distribution of the rainfall, by the humidity of the air, and by the movements of the atmosphere. He referred me to the work of Schimper, a great Swiss botanist who was one of the founders of plant geography. There is an English edition of his book; but it is nearly forty years old, and the latest German edition (1935) has much more information about Mexico.

The Mexican plateau, he says, though on the whole it possesses a dry climate, has generally more rain than the deserts of the United States. Its dryness is chiefly due to the mountain ranges which enclose it to east and west. Warm easterly winds, blowing in from the Mexican Gulf, reach the coast saturated with moisture. So on the eastern slopes of the highlands a tropical vegetation is possible, as is shown particularly in the luxuriant tropical forests of the State of Chiapas. The high plateau, however, gets very little of this moisture. Places in the south of the plateau show an annual rainfall of 20 in. and more, which if it were evenly distributed would be enough for a type of vegetation not needing a great deal of moisture. But, as a matter of fact, three-quarters of this amount of rain falls in about three months, between June and September, and hardly one-eighth during the long, dry period from November to April; so that the total rainfall is apparently not enough, even for a vegetation which does not require a great deal of moisture, on account of the great evaporation which takes place during the drier months. The farther away from the rain-bringing gulf, the more the drought increases; and since sheltered places have a still lower rainfall than those which are exposed to the easterly winds, there are many which go for long periods with practically no rain at all. These include the "plateau deserts" and "semi-deserts", mostly in high-lying regions in which the dryness is affected by the influence of the altitude on the climate, and also by the soil. The soil in these places usually consists of a firm reddish clay, full of stones; in the dry seasons the clay becomes as hard as a rock, and splits into cracks and fissures, so that for all practical purposes it is equivalent to a substratum of real rock.

Then there is the question of dew. The still, tropical night plays an important part in cooling the lower strata of the atmosphere. Owing to radiation, the ground temperature falls considerably, and also the temperature of the layer of air in contact with the ground, so that there can be heavy dew, even in a tropical region, during a period of drought. The daily temperature chart, put up in the Mexico City General Post Office, shows how low the ground temperature can fall, compared with the maximum and minimum shade temperatures registered at 5 ft. from the ground. Observations have been made on the amount of dew in the comparatively rainless parts of Mexico. A plane tree, with from 15 to 20 sq. metres of leaf surface, in one night condensed between 1185 and 1580 grams of water. This becomes still more important for parasitic plants like Spanish moss which in Mexico will grow, or hang, or twine, on any object from a tree to a telegraph wire, and only live on such water as they can absorb from the air.

"The earth hath no fruitfulness", Isaak Walton said, "without showers or dews: for all the herbs, and flowers, and fruit, are produced and thrive by water." This is true even of a dry country like the greater part of Mexico.

Chapter IV

TREES, BOOKSHOPS AND COLONIAL ARCHITECTURE

Mexico City is, surprisingly, a city of bookshops, new as well as secondhand. Spain has lost the cultural hegemony of the Spanish-speaking peoples; and the more enterprising Spanish publishers are now established in America. Yet it is not only American editions that can be found in Mexico: Spanish publications of the eighteenth and nineteenth centuries are there in any numbers. The Alameda, a delightful formal garden with old trees, on the site once used by the Inquisition for burning heretics, is, on one side at any rate, practically lined with secondhand bookshops; while other vendors have stands or merely lay their books on the pavement. On the south, the more fashionable side, there are two secondhand bookshops, as well as the largest and most international bookstore in Mexico—its Bumpus or Brentano. At these establishments, and at numerous others in the older part of the city, one could find innumerable editions of all sorts and sizes of books printed in Spain; and I was able to fill up many gaps in my library at home.

On my first morning in Mexico, then, as I went out into the Alameda, the first things that struck me were the secondhand bookshops. Then the trees. They were rather dried up: December is in the dry season. A few had lost their leaves; but there were plenty which had not, like the graceful pepper trees—called *pirules*—which will always remain in my mind as the characteristic trees of all seasons in Mexico. As a matter of fact, the *arbol del Perú* is not native to Mexico at all; as its name implies, it came from Peru. In Mexico, it was first grown in the middle of the sixteenth century, from seed sent by Antonio de Mendoza, first Viceroy, after his translation to Peru. The fruit is snapped up by birds,[1] and easily propagated; and to-day it is the tree most often seen in most parts of Mexico, on open stony flats, on plains and mountains; it fits in so well with the landscape and the general appearance of the vegetation, that it is difficult to imagine Mexico without it.

The Alameda and other squares in Mexico City are full of trees, most of them large and well grown. That, too, was unexpected in Mexico; for the protection of trees needs special attention in all towns, and more than ever in towns which are Spanish; and in a country which has had nearly twenty years of unrest and civil war, as Mexico has, it is astonishing that the trees should be so well looked after. Not only the Alameda, but the Jardín de San Fernando, the Plaza de San Juan, and numerous other squares, have large shady trees and gardens; while there are also fine, tree-lined avenues, such as the Paseo de la Reforma, Avenida de Chapultepec, Avenida Insurgentes.

Old Dr Reiche, a German botanist who lived for many years in Mexico City and was formerly professor in the University, used to say that Mexico and its suburbs should be called "the city of ash trees". There are also eucalyptus and cypress; willow, poplar, araucaria, acacia and plane. There is a tree with finger-shaped leaves and stiff tufts of flowers; numerous palms (which flower in Mexico City, but do not fruit), *Sophora*, *Myoporum* (from Australia), *Grevillea*, *Lagunaria*, *Eriobotrya*, and a Japanese privet. Among climbing plants the most usual is *Bougainvillea* in several shades (which can never fail to remind a traveller in Spain of Málaga), *Cobaea* and, more rarely, *Solandra*, with many different kinds of honeysuckle, *Tecoma*, *Ipomoea* and Virginia creeper. The chief ornamental plants are roses, fuchsias, jasmine, heliotrope: with the more exotic cannas, gladiolus, Madonna

[1] Chiefly the Cedar bird.

lilies; red-hot pokers, *Clivia*, *Agapanthus*, snapdragons, nasturtiums, delphiniums, several different kinds of geraniums (some of them climbers), and violets, as well as strange plants from the tropical and subtropical zones of Mexico. Mexico (at least, whenever I have been there) never failed to be full of flowers.

The next striking things in Mexico City—one begins to notice them already from the Alameda—are the buildings in styles which are usually described as "colonial", and constructed of a material which looks like pink pumice-stone. It has an Aztec name, *tezontle*; and that perhaps should bring one to a most remarkable fact about modern Mexico—that Aztec and many of the other aboriginal languages are not dead. They live on both in the fifty or so Indian languages spoken to-day, and in the large number of Aztec words and "Aztecisms" (with smaller numbers of words and "isms" from Maya and Tarascan) which are used constantly in the modern Spanish of Mexico.

Aztequismos! It was not long before I secured a dictionary of them—one of those roughly and provincially printed books of the beginning of the present century, full of curious and discursive learning; and friends afterwards put me in the way of more recent studies of Aztec roots and "Aztecisms" in modern Spanish. I have described *tezontle* as pink pumice-stone, which may not be very accurate, but is as near as I can get to it. The Aztec word means "stone of hairs", *te* (for *tetl*) stone, and *tzontli* hair, "alluding to the fact that, owing to its porous nature, it seems a tangle of petrified hair". It is a volcanic stone, porous yet durable; and the Spaniards, like the Aztecs before them, made great use of it as building material. The chief quarry was afterwards pointed out to me on the road to Puebla, soon after leaving Lake Texcoco, just as the road begins to go up into the hills.

The first colonial buildings of pink *tezontle* which appear from the Alameda are a couple of churches. It is not the fault of impiety or neglect that they seem rather bedraggled. They are crooked, because the soil has subsided; and, having nothing of the tradition of the leaning tower of Pisa, and no memory of any Mexican Galileo making physical experiments from their towers, they are not at all picturesque, and merely look rather untidy. Modern Mexican artists have little use for the picturesque, *lo pintoresco*. One of them has referred to "the exquisite vulgarity of the leaning tower of Pisa, and of the Venus of Milo, who ought to have lived in it".

The really admirable buildings of *tezontle* are not the churches but the palaces, the great exception being the Sacristy of the Cathedral, which, alas, has also been sinking, and during both my visits to Mexico was boarded up and unapproachable. The original Spanish buildings of the time of Cortés have all disappeared; even his own house, which occupied an immense area in the middle of the present town, a space equal to several blocks of existing buildings. It was burnt down in 1636, and the site (or a considerable part of it) is now occupied by the "Monte" (i.e. *Monte de piedad*), the National Pawnshop. The sixteenth-century houses which still exist have plain façades without entablatures or cornices; but their flat, outer walls are usually covered with stucco relief: angels, crowns and scrolls, monograms and vases. There are still a few such houses tucked away in what are now poor and unattractive streets.

The making of the city, as a real piece of architecture, was due to the Baroque art of the seventeenth century and the Churrigueresque of the eighteenth; while the peculiar dignity and barbaric elegance of many of the buildings was due to the native Indian workmen. The chief material, as I have said, was pink porous *tezontle*, while border-work and mouldings were of hard grey *chiluca*. *Chiluca* is a stone so called from the place where it was first quarried, a place in the Valley of Mexico formerly celebrated for the abundance, or hotness, of its chili pepper. *Chiluca*, being grey, made an excellent contrast with pink *tezontle*; and the effect when (as not infrequently happens) glazed, coloured tiles are used as well, is pleasant and stimulating, especially on a bright December day, at 7000 ft. above the level of the sea. In the eighteenth century particularly, the thing was to have a corner house and decorate two fronts, the supreme example being the tiled corner house with two fronts on streets and one on a narrow lane—the building now occupied by a well-known department store.

Apart from tiles, there is at least one house with a carved plumed serpent taken from an Aztec temple; while huge gargoyles in the shape of cannon project far over the street, so as not to wet either the front of the house or those passing by underneath. Remains of Aztec temples were built in to churches, as well as private houses. The cathedral is on the site of the Great Pyramid, on the top of which Cortés and his men (so Bernal Díaz says, and he was there) were revolted by the smells left by human sacrifice; and there are still important remains buried in the big main square. Indeed, the Director of the Anthropological Institute believes that he could put his finger (or his spade) on one of them, if only they would let him dig up one corner of the Big Square; but Mexican municipal authorities are not so ready to dig up their streets and squares as their opposite numbers are in London. It is true, at any rate, that the Big Square (el Zócalo) and the buildings round it have provided the principal pieces of Aztec sculpture which are now in the National Museum; and it is natural that this should be so, because the Big Square was originally part of the great court in which were the various buildings forming what the chroniclers call *El Templo Mayor*.

Some of the best colonial buildings are in the four parallel streets which lead from the direction of the Alameda to the Big Square: but there are many others, and in wandering about the older parts of Mexico City, you never can tell where there will not be an attractive colonial house. They are all built round patios, of course, and the patios are sometimes open to everyone, without the bother of asking permission or an authorized guide. The best of these is the patio of the sumptuous palace in the Avenida Madero, with a strikingly decorative façade, and an immense doorway. It is an eighteenth-century palace, which in the 1820's belonged to Iturbide; and it was from there—through that uncommonly high door—that he went to be crowned Emperor of Mexico, after the war of independence. The crown (an eyewitness reports) was delivered in a hamper, as if it was a Christmas turkey. (But what would you pack a crown in?) A hundred years ago, in 1839, when Madame Calderón de la Barca saw the palace, it was already falling to ruins; but afterwards it was thoroughly (if not always very fortunately) repaired, and now the ground floor is a bank and the other floors are let as offices. It is well kept; and has the advantage already stated, that anyone can go into the courtyard without being stopped (or feeling that he may be stopped) and asked what his business is.

I am not attempting to write a guide-book. If I were, I should have to describe many other Mexican houses of the colonial period; for in Mexico City, as in Puebla, the houses are generally more beautiful and more interesting than the churches. There is, for instance, the attractive pair of corner houses near the Museum: Nos. 18, 20 and 22 of the Calle de la Moneda, at the corner which used to be known as "The Sorrowful Indian", *El Indio Triste*. They are built of pink *tezontle* with the windows framed in greyish white *chiluca*; while facing one another, at the two corners, are square towers, each with a niche and a statue on the corner, looking diagonally across the street. Such rooms built on the roof are still found in other old Mexican houses, and were called the Watchman's Room, *Cuarto del Velador*.

The National Library of Mexico (like many libraries in the provinces), was formerly a church. Mexico, like Spain, somewhat overbuilt itself in the way of churches; and the plan of turning superfluous conventicles into public libraries is one that might be followed in other countries besides Mexico.

Not all the fine old buildings of the colonial period are palaces. There are several examples of early housing schemes for people in humble circumstances. Nos. 108 to 138 in the Calle de San Jerónimo (formerly known, grimly enough, as the Street of the Good Death, *Calle de la Buena Muerte*) form an eighteenth-century building for families of small means; outwardly, at any rate, it shows considerable dignity and sense of proportion. The same is true of the houses numbered 8, 10 and 12 in the narrow street of the Tobacconists, *Tabaqueros*; and the much more interesting and beautiful one in the Calle de Mesones (No. 119), which has the doors and windows framed in broad bands of whitish *chiluca* going right up to the cornice.

Though the old building of the famous sixteenth-century college of San Juan de Tlaltelolco has almost gone, and the eighteenth-century alterations as well, there is still said to be a gallery inside (which I did not see) with pointed arches belonging to the original college building. The survival of pointed arches in a few early sixteenth-century buildings in Mexico is a fact of considerable interest. The eighteenth-century Jesuit college, Colegio Máximo de San Ildefonso, still exists, serving a more useful purpose as the National Preparatory School, Escuela Nacional Preparatoria. The fine façade is of pink *tezontle* and whitish *chiluca*; there are spacious courts and high doorways. Not far off is the *tezontle* building founded as the Hospicio de San Nicolás, and converted as long ago as 1792 into a School of Mining Engineering; while the present National Conservatoire of Music is an interesting eighteenth-century house in the same neighbourhood, once the residence of a wealthy family (Calle de la Moneda, 14 and 16); such as lived also in the house (Justo Sierra, 19) now the seat of the Mexican Geographical Society, with its original façade, and courts with galleries running round the first story, and supported by columns.

The immense and imposing Palacio Nacional, the official residence of the President of the Republic, is also mainly in the colonial style; so is the National School of Medicine, the site of the Tribunal of the Inquisition. The Ministry of Education and Fine Arts is a seventeenth-century building erected on the site of a convent of the Incarnation, founded in 1594 by Conceptionist nuns.

It takes more than one morning's wandering through streets which are noisy and grimy, but always at right angles to one another, to track down the remains of the characteristic colonial style in Mexico City. Two of the best monuments of this period I have not yet mentioned, and they lie rather far apart. One is an arcaded square, the Plaza de Santo Domingo, which dates from about 1685. The building with the arcades shows the typical colonial characteristics, particularly the form of window frame, so noticeable afterwards at Puebla, with the jambs prolonged so as to reach the cornice. There is a pleasant garden in the middle of the square; while under the arcades are the public letter-writers, taking down (on typewriters) letters for those who cannot read or write. The same thing used to be found at Barcelona, and at Naples: but the presence of typewriters was unexpected; it showed that one was no longer in Europe but in America.

The other colonial building of great interest is Las Vizcaínas, a baroque building begun in 1734, as the Colegio de San Ignacio, and now the home of numerous poor families. On the way to this lies yet one more colonial house, one of the most beautiful in the whole of Mexico City, the building now occupied by the National Bank of Mexico in the Street of Isabel la Católica.

Once again, if this were a guide-book, it would have to describe the innumerable and striking wall-paintings by Diego Rivera, Orozco, and others, which decorate and enliven all manner of Mexican public buildings, new and old; the Presidential Palace, numerous government offices, the National University and the Airport. There is no need for me to do so, because American books describing and illustrating them have already been published in England. The most accurate and unbiased accounts of modern Mexico were all published originally in the United States.

Here, it will be enough to say that the contemporary school of Mexican mural painters aims at making Mexican history and Mexican life intelligible to the large number of those who do not read history because they cannot read at all. I forget what the figures for illiteracy in Mexico are; but they are higher even than in Spain, and they are increased by people who have learned to read with difficulty—in middle life, perhaps—and for whom reading is still the laborious deciphering of confusing signs, many of which are very like one another, and are often too small and too badly printed to be easily distinguished. I have had the same experience myself, in trying in middle life to learn languages with strange alphabets, and am still in the stage of laboriously spelling out the words and wishing the type were larger, as it is in books for children. To Mexicans who cannot read, and especially to Indians, mural paintings are particularly appropriate: for their ancestors, as everybody knows, had a form of picture-writing; and archaeologists have told me that when it is a question of deciphering an Aztec or Maya inscription in hieroglyphics, the illiterate native will often see, much more quickly than the educated researcher, what object a hieroglyph is supposed to represent. Later on, when I used to spend mornings in the National Museum, it was the brown people—partly or wholly Indian (and they were always to be seen wandering round the Museum just as I was)—who could see what the sculpture or the picture-written manuscripts really were about.

So it is unnecessary to say anything more about the modern Mexican historical frescoes, and it is beside the point for me to say which churches I looked into, in the hope—a hope that was often disappointed—of finding a splendid Baroque or Churrigueresque gilt retablo. The hope was disappointed because so much Churrigueresque carving has disappeared. This is not the work of the "godless" revolutionaries; it was the deliberate act of the ecclesiastics themselves. In the nine-teenth century and the twentieth as well, such gorgeous works of art—and they are most enthralling, those that remain—were held to distract the faithful from their devotions; so they were replaced by tons of Carrara marble and white and gold paint generally executed by Italians, who must have made fortunes out of it. In many churches this "Lourdes style" has entirely replaced the style of Churriguera. The Church, like everything else in the nineteenth century (and in other cen-turies), felt differently from the century before; and the "old religion", which is certainly the newest in its eagerness not to be far behind the times, had to bring churches into line with nineteenth-century ideas of decoration; to be in keeping with an age which (as a musical historian has expressed it) "proclaimed the dogma of the Immaculate Conception, and invented the harmonium to sing its praises". The *harmonium*, of all instruments!

But that brings me to music; and on the evening of my first day in Mexico City there was a concert of contemporary Mexican music. It was an orchestral concert, held in the National Palace of Fine Arts (*Bellas Artes*, for short), and sponsored by the Board of Education. The conductor was Maestro Silvestre Revueltas, whom I had heard at a concert at Valencia, in August 1937, one Sunday morning during the Spanish war. Revueltas appeared now as the composer of *Música para charlar* (a conversation-piece) also described as "Scenes from a Film". It was a lively, modern composition; but being written for a film—and a film of progress, road-making, and colonization in Lower California—the ideas, motives, visions, never returned, and the work was without form, though by no means void. In some ways I liked it better than the other work of Revueltas—it was less aggressive, at any rate than his negroid symphonic poem. This had three movements: "Caminos", "Sensemaya" (a magic song for destroying a serpent) and "Janitzio". These were full of stuff and vitality, and had a sense of form, especially notable in the song for killing a snake, which closely followed a poem by the negro poet, Nicolás Guillén, or at least reproduced the alternation of magic nonsense verses with verses which had (in the ordinary sense of the word) meaning. I also liked *Zapotlán*, a slighter but very agreeable symphonic suite by Maestro Rolón, based on memories of the music of his childhood. The remaining piece was *Merlin*, a symphonic suite from an opera of Albéniz, orchestrated (and rather pepped up) by Maestro Ponce. It was a capable piece of work, but hardly made the Albéniz of that period come alive. I afterwards went to most of the Symphony Concerts conducted by Carlos Chávez between July and September, and attended some of his rehearsals. He has created an excellent orchestra and gives very interesting programmes, in which a good deal of time is given to contemporary music.

Coming out of the concert I found a monument to Beethoven, presented to the city of Mexico by the German colony, in the first months of depression and disillusion after the war of 1914–19. I know that if the Germans had won that war, they would have tried to restore a Mexican dictatorship under a nephew of Porfirio Díaz; but that is not the point. To present a monument to Beethoven: how typically German; but how splendidly German, too! To cling to late Beethoven quartets in a moment of national abasement, misery and hunger! But that was as natural as it is for good Spaniards to cling to their painting, poetry and music, in conditions even more tragical than those that befell Germany. The good Germans in those days were not Nazis but *Wandervögel*, who might have saved Europe (just as the Spanish Liberals might) if they had been properly supported in other countries.

A little farther down the Alameda is a rose garden, which ought to have been presented by the British Colony as a monument to Shakespeare. But I am afraid the British Colony in Mexico has generally expected Mexicans to pay for anything which has been done for them, and pay through the nose for it, too. Sometimes, when I am abroad and alone,

I think that when all our engineering and trade and colonization have been forgotten—yes, and even our science, too—England may be remembered as a country of poets. For some years I have been telling people so, and have always been met with polite incredulity. Yet the more I read poetry in various languages, the more I come back, with wonder and amazement, to poetry in English. Of course there will be irresistible totalitarian pressure in favour of another language; while the difficulty of English (when it comes to poetry), and above all the extreme difficulty of our greatest poet, whether in his own language or translated, will probably reduce the public for Shakespeare to the size of the public for the late Beethoven quartets. But that, at any rate, will be something.

Chapter V

PYRAMIDS

The next day happened to be my birthday; and my friends (though fortunately unaware of that fact) celebrated it by an excursion to the most famous archaeological site near Mexico City: Teotihuacán.[1] Teotihuacán was built by the Toltecs; and though they were once explained to me by no less an authority than T. A. Joyce, I found it difficult to remember at first exactly where the Toltecs came in. Dr Spinden, a famous Americanist and author of one of those excellent handbooks published by the American Museum of Natural History, *American Civilizations of Mexico and Central America*, simplifies the relationship of the leading races in ancient Mexico, by a curious analogy from the early history of Europe. He draws a parallel between the Mayas and Aztecs in the New World and the Greeks and Romans in the Old—a parallel which holds good at any rate as regards their relations to one another. The Mayas of Yucatán and a large part of Central America were an artistic and intellectual people, who developed sculpture, painting, architecture, music, astronomy, and other arts and sciences. They were able to do so because of their plentiful food-supply and easy conditions of life which allowed them the leisure to become civilized. Like the Greeks, they were divided into numerous communities and small states, which were always quarrelling with one another. Temporary leagues were formed, and broken, between the larger cities; but real unity was only possible against a common enemy. Culturally, however, the

[1] *Te-ó-ti wa-kán*; do | do : . re : ti | do.

3-2

Mayas, like the Greeks, were one people. In spite of their different dialects they had a common language which is still spoken to-day by the quarter of a million people in Yucatán, and is even said to be making progress at the expense of Spanish; and (again, like the Greeks) the ancient Mayas were bound together by a common religion and a common mode of thought. The religion of the Mayas was, needless to say, a great deal more barbarous than that of the Greeks—in classical times, at any rate. Even the Greeks had uncomfortable memories of human sacrifice (Iphigenia, for instance): and there is not much difference in being offered up on an altar and ceremonially burnt in the Greek manner, than in being anointed and massaged, dressed in one's best clothes and jewels, and thrown into a well, as happened among the Mayas of Yucatán. Where Greeks and Mayas come nearest one another is not in their attitude to human sacrifice, but in their feeling that their mythology and beliefs, hopes and fears, might be idealized and beautified in art.

So if the Mayas may in certain respects be compared with the Greeks, the Aztecs will seem more like the Romans, a "brusque and warlike people", conquerors and administrators, whose language spread with their conquests, but who could have done nothing without the ruins of an earlier civilization to build upon, though they destroyed that civilization by force of arms, before they made their most notable contributions to Mexican life in the arts of organization and government.

The Toltecs come just before the Aztecs, and may be compared with the Etruscans. They had a culture derived, in part at any rate, from their brilliant contemporaries, the Mayas; and this culture was magnified to something approaching greatness by their ruder but better organized successors.

The principal Toltec site is Teotihuacán; and the idea among archaeologists to-day is that the "Tula" from which the Toltecs are supposed to have taken their name was not the rather insignificant ruin of that name on the north edge of the Valley of Mexico, but Teotihuacán itself. The Toltecs appear early in prehistoric Mexico, in the remains of primitive man which have been discovered under the Pedregal—the old lava bed which is now (in the right season) a paradise of wild flowers—south-west of Mexico City. Toltec objects lie just above those of the Archaic period; but even so, the schemes of decoration on their pots show a relationship with the earlier and more brilliant work of the Mayas; while their pyramids, if bigger, were not so well constructed, and the temples on the top so flimsy that not a single one is standing.

One of the most curious things about the Toltecs was their ball-game. I afterwards saw one of the courts in which it was played, in Yucatán. The game was part of their religion; though whether they had a saying "It's not ball-game!" and used it with the same ethical and moral significance as "It's not cricket!" the authorities do not say.

But the Toltecs left one fatal legacy to modern Mexico. They invented *pulque*, that malodorous and discouraging drink, made from the fermented juice of the agave mixed with milk which has turned sour. *Pulque* is the great problem of modern Mexico, the rock on which so many urgent reforms are shattered and brought to nothing. The *pulque* industry is a huge vested interest; acres and acres are cultivated with nothing beyond the prickly agave plant from which the juice is extracted, and the finished product seems to produce a form of alcoholism which is peculiarly demoralizing and brutalizing in its results. While I was in Mexico, fresh and renewed efforts were being made by the Government of the devoted and untiring President Cárdenas to check the evil of *pulque*. Of course, Mexico is a thirsty country. No one can be surprised that people of all classes should want to drink, and no one could blame them for occasionally drinking too much; but the stuff they drink is often deplorable. The best local product seems to be a light beer of the Pilsener type, known as Bohemia; but what seems most in demand, in various forms, is either *pulque* or practically raw spirit. Efforts to check the sale of these were being directed more especially to the factory towns; *cantinas*, *piqueras*, cabarets and all the different varieties of tavern were being closed, so that their finances might be inquired into. It was interesting to see where the vested interests lay. At Ciudad Juárez, on the United States border, the capital invested in the liquor trade was mainly American, while most of the important Mexicans in the town were said to live on the profits of alcoholism and "centres of vice". In most other centres, however, these things were in the hands of Spaniards—not republicans but *gachupines*, those get-rich-quick Spaniards, firm supporters of the Right, whose occupation in Mexico is best described as that of middleman, and could probably be dispensed with. (That is one of the reasons why the refugees from the war—who are mainly workers—have been so welcome.) The *gachupines*, in complicity with certain Mexicans, who also lived by exploitation, are as a rule those who sell *pulque* in Mexico City, and install *cantinas* all over the towns. In a street in which there is a school, there are likely to be two or three taverns; while in the neighbourhood of a factory it is calculated that there are on an average three *pulquerías* and perhaps a *vinatería* as well, a place which sells the most poisonous liquor at the lowest prices.

Of course, the thought of suppression, of closing the *pulquerías*, raises the outcry of "Trampling on legitimate rights"; and every dodge will be employed to bring the well-meaning attempts of President Cárdenas to nothing. Bootleggers have been out of employment for so many years, that prospects in Mexico may induce them to return to the business.

Here I should like to make a humble suggestion. Mexico is not by any means the only country in the world which has suffered from alcoholism. Even the best-governed countries suffered, including one of the best-run countries there is: Sweden. My proposal would be that the Mexican Government should study the way in which this problem has been dealt with by Sweden (if indeed they have not done so already), and invite one or two Swedish social workers to Mexico, to study conditions for themselves and suggest how they may be improved. Swedish social workers are among the foremost in the world of to-day. In Spain, in Abyssinia, in any place where there was self-sacrificing work to be done for the good of humanity, there have always been one or two Swedes (I remember them well in Valencia); and the Swedish nation, having suffered and overcome a ticklish problem of alcoholism in its own country, would, I am sure, be ready to offer the most sensible, expert advice as to how the evil in Mexico might be remedied. Another suggestion would be to follow the plan proposed in Spain by Don Francisco Giner, for dealing with a bad school: to open a better one opposite. In front of every *pulquería*, the Government might open a place for the sale of good, cheap beer.

So if it was the Toltecs who discovered how to make *pulque*, they have much to answer for in retarding Mexican civilization. They are accused of other unfortunate practices as well. They took to war and spoliation as a means of building up tribal wealth. There had been war in Central America before their time, but not a war of conquest with a view to aggrandizement. The Toltecs lived in a part of the country less favoured than the Mayas; and it may have been the consequence of pressure of population combined with the less abundant food-supply of an arid country, which drove the Toltecs to attack other countries with a food-supply abundant enough to release many persons from the pursuit of producing food to that of art and science.

The importance of the Toltecs lies mainly in their mythology. In the legendary history of Mexico, as told by the Mexicans themselves in their manuscripts and picture-books, the old Toltec myths come first; and it was the Toltecs who evolved the poetic figure of Quetzalcoatl.[1] The name of Quetzalcoatl will be familiar to all readers of modern English from *The Plumed Serpent* of D. H. Lawrence; and I maintain that that

[1] *Ke-tsal-kwa-tl*, | do : re : mi : do |.

work, and *Mexico: A Study of Two Americas* by Stuart Chase, are the two most enlightening and indispensable books on Mexico to-day. Quetzalcoatl is an example of the priest-king who becomes a god. He was one of the three great rulers of the Toltecs. He worked out a calendar for them, a simpler form of the calendar of the Mayas; and it was he who led the Toltec expedition which captured the more or less holy Maya city of Chichén Itzá. Spinden thinks that the historical Quetzalcoatl spent his youth in Yucatán, and returned to his highland home with strange new religious and social ideas. He was against human sacrifice (which led to a war of religion between the "old believers" and the reformers), and he eventually founded Cholula as a centre for his reformed and less barbarous religion.

But it is a mistake to treat fable and legend with the calm detachment of a historian inquiring into the origins of a war. Legend has an appropriate literary form; and I should like to quote some of the story of Quetzalcoatl from a book of Mexican fairy-tales, published not long ago by Srta Amelia Martínez del Río (who is, incidentally, a trained archaeologist, and one of the assistant curators of the Mexican National Museum), *The Sun, the Moon, and a Rabbit* (New York, 1935). I quote this book, because Srta Martínez del Río has put the old Mexican legends into far better English than I can.

Once there was a king called "Plumed Serpent".
Nobody knows where he came from.
Some say he might have been a strayed Irish priest.
Some say he might have been Saint Thomas, the Apostle.
Some say he came from the Sea, because he used a big conch shell as a horn.
Nevertheless, he was a white man with a long white beard. He was dressed in a long white tunic embroidered with red crosses.
He was king of the Toltec people about the time the pyramids were built.
Plumed Serpent was good.
He was a great lover of peace and a great lover of agriculture.

During his reign corn grew twice as big and pumpkins achieved the size of a man.

He taught his people many things.

He knew about the stars and how they moved in the heavens.... He knew how to measure time and so invented the calendar, one more perfect by far than the one the Spaniards had when they came.

He taught his people the art of carving stones and melting metals.

He was wise and prudent and a law-maker.

He reigned over the Toltec people until he was eighty years old.[1]

But there was a great magician, "as wicked as he was wise": the god "Smoking Mirror", Tezcatlipoca. Smoking Mirror and Plumed Serpent had always been enemies. Just as Plumed Serpent was a lover of peace and stopped his ears with cotton when he heard men speak of war, Smoking Mirror loved war and vengeance and black magic. At last, with lies and magic he made Plumed Serpent drink wine of the agave (*pulque*) which made him drunk. After that, Plumed Serpent—like Noah—was despised by his followers and had to abandon his kingdom. So he burned his palaces and his carpets of precious feathers. But before he left, he made a prophecy—he would return.

"Know that there will come men with beards and with their heads covered with basins of metal.

"They will come from the East and over the waves of the sea, and these white and bearded men will take from you the rule of this land of mine; they will give you another god."...

His heart was heavy—he knew his end was near. So he made a big fire and threw himself into the flames.

His faithful ones chanted farewell.

When his body began to burn, a column of smoke rose to the heavens. Birds of precious feathers flew around it, and his heart was seen to rise to the sky. There it was transformed to a star which began to shine at that moment—this is the Evening Star.

[1] He also (according to Mendieta, *Historia ecclesiástica indiana*, 1596) went down to the world of the dead to collect the bones of past generations, and created humanity afresh by pouring over them his own blood.

So Plumed Serpent became a god, next in importance to the Sun and the Moon; and at Teotihuacán, in the citadel, a temple was built to him, and decorated with the beautiful feathered snake.

Everyone will remember how the old Indian belief in the return of Quetzalcoatl helped Cortés in his conquest; for, like a good empire builder, he was quite ready to make use of the legend and pose as Quetzalcoatl himself. Even as lately as the sixties of the last century, the tradition of a fair-bearded stranger from across the sea was used in an attempt to sway Indian sentiment in favour of Maximilian; and the makers of the admirable film, *Juárez*, have introduced a good, if unconscious piece of mythology, in making a white bird fly up from the smoke in which the Emperor's body fell before the firing-party at Querétaro.

Archaeology is taken very seriously in modern Mexico; moreover, it is the one Mexican subject on which good modern books have been published in England. So there is no need for me to put my foot in it—in any sense—and express opinions on a subject in which I have no special training. Teotihuacán at any rate is the greatest monument of the Toltecs still visible to-day. My impressions of it are that it must have been a big city, full of magnificent buildings. It is still an immense place—something like four miles long by two miles wide. The ruins consist of pyramids and courts symmetrically arranged according to a complicated astronomical plan. Each temple was so situated that (as at Stonehenge) the first rays of the rising sun would strike a certain part of it on a certain day of the year; and the whole city was apparently a great religious centre. At one end is the Pyramid of the Moon (not yet excavated); in the middle is the Pyramid of the Sun, and at the other end the Temple of Quetzalcoatl. All the way along the main road (named, for some reason, the Highway of the Dead) are a number of smaller heaps of stones and pyramids, most of them not yet excavated. The Pyramid of the Sun is over 200 ft. high, constructed in five big steps, with a wide stairway up the west side—easy enough to go up, but the very devil to come down, unless you have a remarkably good head (which I have not). The stairs led originally to a little chapel of the sun-god; but the image was, of course, thrown down by that zealous destroyer of idols and manuscripts, Archbishop Zumárraga.

The Temple of Quetzalcoatl is later, and of rather different design; it consists of a large court, surrounded by platforms and smaller pyramids with the temple in the middle. This is smaller than those of the Sun and Moon; but contains some astonishing and beautiful sculpture of plumed serpents, swimming about among sea-shells. Joyce says that they were symbolic of the ripple of wind on water. The sight of it suggested feathers, and the movement, that of a sea-serpent.

On the way to Teotihuacán we stopped at a ruined but restored monastery—San Agustín de Acolmán, near Tepexpán. It was not destroyed in an anti-religious revolution, or even by the *cristeros*. Floods, in the eighteenth century, were responsible, and the gradual rise in the level of the ground to about 12 ft. higher than it was before. The buildings have now been excavated: and we saw an admirable two-storied cloister, a church and a library with the yellow, parchment-covered books being put back in their places.

The moment we got back there was a Gargantuan lunch—Gargantuan, but otherwise very agreeable, at the Asturian Club (*Centro Asturiano*). In December 1938 the war in Spain was still undecided, and good Spaniards, though exiles, were not yet refugees. At one moment the conversation—and it was a real conversation of exiles—turned on the name of a certain street in Madrid, connecting the Calle Mayor with the Calle del Arenal. I happened to know the street well (there was a good secondhand bookshop in it), and I even remembered its name, though it would have been indecent for a stranger to have butted in—above a whisper—when so many Spanish people who had known Madrid well were racking their brains to remember.

Chapter VI

TOLTEC LEGENDS

If Teotihuacán is one of the greatest archaeological centres of Mexico, it is also a great centre for mythology. The name means "where the gods dwell", and it was there that they met to decide what was to be done at various stages of the creation. I have always had a preference for legends rather than for more sober history, and (as once in Spain, so now in Mexico) I found legend a very pleasant guide; indeed legend is essential when it comes to the main exhibits in the Mexican National Museum.

The famous Aztec calendar stone, for instance. That stone is not only a marvellous piece of decorative art; it shows why the gods met at Teotihuacán, and what they decided to do. The stone is round and about 12 ft. across. In the middle is the face of the sun god—of the god who is in charge of the sun now, or was in charge of it when the Spaniards captured the city of Mexico and overthrew the great temple in 1521. Round the face of the god are four squares, each one framing a symbol which represents one of the four gods who have had charge of the sun in the past, and one of the four great catastrophes which, on four separate occasions, have overwhelmed the whole race of man.

In the highest heaven (the legend says) lived a god and a goddess who were the most powerful of all the gods. They had many children, of whom the most distinguished were Plumed Serpent (Quetzalcoatl) and Smoking Mirror (Tezcatlipoca), and these were made lords of creation. They managed to create half a sun; but as it did not give enough light, Smoking

Chichén Itzá (*Yucatán*)*: Toltec Ball-court*
(*See p.* 94)

Mexico: Aztec Calendar Stone

Mirror was himself made into a sun, and wandered round the sky for 676 years, while on earth the only human beings were giants who were too ignorant to till the soil. At last, Smoking Mirror was knocked down by his brother, Plumed Serpent. So he turned into a jaguar and ate up the giants. There were great earthquakes, and more jaguars came down from the mountains and ate up the rest of mankind.

Then Plumed Serpent became Sun, and ruled the sky for 364 years until Smoking Mirror brought him down with a blow from his paw. A great wind got up; trees were blown down, and all mankind perished except some who grew tails and became monkeys, and could hold on to the few remaining trees so fast that they were not blown away.

Then the rain god (Tlaloc) became Sun; but either he resigned (as one version has it) or was brought down by Plumed Serpent, who made him rain fire, so that men perished or were turned into birds. He was succeeded by his wife, or sister, Jade Skirts (Chalchiutlícue); but some god—it was probably Smoking Mirror—made it rain so hard that the earth was flooded, and men perished or were turned into fishes.

Then the sky itself fell down; and Smoking Mirror and Plumed Serpent had to hold it up, so that the earth could see the sun once more. The last sun had got lost in the fall of the sky, and there was no one left to be the light of the world. Things were left in darkness for twenty-five years, when the gods all met again at Teotihuacán and decided to create another sun. One of themselves, they agreed, must sacrifice himself; so the poorest and unhappiest offered to do so, jumped into a fire, and thus became the fifth and present sun, which will rule until, on a certain day already determined, it will end in an earthquake.

Another version of the creation of the last sun was collected by Padre Sahagún in the sixteenth century. He wrote it down in Aztec, just as it was told him, and his version was only translated into Spanish in the nineteenth century.

First the Sun came out, and then the moon. And those who tell
stories say that at first their light was equal: but when the gods saw
that they shone with equal brightness, they spoke once more with
one another and said: "O Gods! How shall this be? Is it good that
they go level? Is it well that they shine with equal light?" So the
gods gave sentence, and said: "Let it be in this wise." And one
of them ran and threw a rabbit in the moon's face, and darkened
his face and dulled its brightness, and his face remained as it is
now.

What we know as the Man in the Moon, the Mexicans see as
a rabbit.

But though the sun was there, it stuck on the rim of the sky.
The gods asked what was the matter now; and were told that
they must all sacrifice themselves as well. One of them
(Evening Star) shot an arrow at the sun, like a ray of light;
but the sun caught it, and sent it back so that Evening Star
was killed and all the other gods (who by this time had
become stars) as well, the last to go being Morning Star,
Evening Star's twin brother; for the Evening Star is sometimes
the first of the stars to disappear before the rising sun, and at
other times the last.

Each of the four catastrophes which have overwhelmed the
Aztec universe was known by the name of the sun which was
ruling at the time: Jaguar sun, Wind sun, Fire sun and Water
sun; and these are shown symbolically in the four squares
round the face of the fifth and present sun in the middle of the
stone calendar. There are two other signs in the inner ring of
the stone; on each side are eagle's claws (or, as I rather see
them, an eagle's eye and beak) holding a human heart; for
the sun in the morning is an eagle ascending, and in the
evening an eagle falling—Eagle falling, *Cuauhtémoc*, the name
which, with wonderful poetic foresight, was given to the last
Aztec emperor.

The second ring is divided into twenty oblong compart-
ments, in each of which is the name, the symbol, of one of the
twenty days of the Aztec month: Alligator day, Wind day,

House day, Lizard day, Serpent day, Death day, Deer day, Rabbit day, Water day, Dog day, Monkey day, Grass day, Reed day, Jaguar day, Eagle day, Vulture day, Movement day, Flint day, Rain day and Flower day. There were eighteen months of these twenty days, and five additional "Days that do not count", which were always looked upon as unlucky.

Surrounding the circle of days is another ring, composed of little squares with what look like five "pips" in each. They are the hieroglyphs for *jade*, as being the most precious thing the Aztecs had, and therefore a symbol of the sun.

Outside this narrow ring is a broad ring, made up of several different parts, and interrupted at eight different places by large, V-shaped signs, which are the sun's rays. There is, first, a ring of eagle's feathers, then the representation of a leather band adorned with jade stones; edging this band is a hiero-glyph of drops of blood; for the gods (it was held) having given their blood for men, expected men to shed their blood for the gods in the sacrifice of human victims.

Surrounding all the other symbols, and forming the extreme outer circle, are two burning, fiery serpents. Their heads face one another at the bottom of the stone; their bodies are divided into sections by the symbol of flame; while inside the open mouth of each serpent is the face of a god. At the top of the circle, between the fiery serpents' tails, is a square containing the date when the fifth and existing sun was created.

These strange, poetic fancies of Aztec and Toltec mytho-logy gave infinite scope to Indian story-tellers. They were particularly fond of the four suns and the four disasters, as may be seen in *The Sun, the Moon and a Rabbit* by Srta Martínez del Río.

In the city of Teotihuacán there lived a newly married couple. One evening this man and woman sat by the fire of their hearth and gazed into the flames.

Suddenly from the flames sprang an old and wrinkled man who

told them that a terrible disaster would afflict mankind. He said that volcanoes would vomit rivers of lava and that a devastating fire would rain from the sky. The wrinkled god said:

"All mankind but you two shall perish. Take with you the fire of your hearth, and hide in yonder cave. The gods love you because of your faithfulness, and will save you so that mankind will not disappear."

The disaster came, as had been foretold, and men were swallowed up by the burning lava. "Oh gods, that we were birds!" they cried; and instantly millions of birds filled the sky.

This seems to be an embroidered version of the Fire sun. The Water sun forms the subject of other stories.

A Toltec version of the destruction of the fourth sun brings before us "Seven Snake", a young and beautiful goddess who was the goddess of agriculture. She was bidden to destroy mankind for the fourth time, because of their wickedness; they were forgetting the gods. She went home and talked to her friends, the gods of Rain, Wind and Fire. Meanwhile, the Earth grew barren; the harvest dried up; men were starving. Eventually jaguars came down from the mountains and devoured the evil race of mortals.

Then Seven Snake returned, with Rain, Fire and Wind in the form of gentle breezes. Flowers and corn sprang up; for it was, of course, the return of Spring. The catastrophe brought on by the young goddess was called Earth sun. But the sun refused to shine, skies remained black and sombre until, in Teotihuacán, the gods created a new sun. The smallest and ugliest of them jumped into the fire, followed by a braver and nobler god, whom the Aztecs afterwards identified as Huitzilopochtli.

Huitzilopochtli became the god of war; but he was originally the sun, the young warrior born every morning from the womb of Mother Earth (or of "Serpent-skirt", Coatlicue, mother of the gods), and dying every evening, so as to take his light to the world of the dead. As soon as he is born, he has to fight his brothers, the stars, and his sister the moon; every day, armed with a sun ray he puts them to flight, and his victory signifies a new day of life for man. The victory won, he is carried in triumph to the mid-point of the sky by the souls of dead warriors fallen in battle or on the stone of sacrifice. When afternoon begins, he is received by the souls of women dead in childbirth, who are equal to warriors because they died in taking a man prisoner—the newly born male child. During the afternoon, the souls of the mothers lead the sun towards his setting, where the stars die and where the sun himself (like the eagle) falls and dies and is received once more by the earth. So the Aztecs were the people of Huitzilopochtli, the people chosen by the sun.[1]

That the Aztecs came to Mexico from the north, there can be no doubt. There is archaeological evidence, and also linguistic evidence: one or two isolated groups of Indians in North America still speak languages allied to Aztec, and so do other Indians, in the north of Mexico.

According to the legends, the Aztecs came from the Land of Herons (Aztlan), or the Land Surrounded by Water (Atlan). In a lake of blue water was an island with a mountain on it, and the top of the mountain was shaped like an eagle's beak. A man and a woman came in a canoe, and settled on the island. At first their children were dumb; but a dove came, perched in an *ahuehuete* tree, and taught them to speak. When eventually the island became too crowded, the god Mexi (the humming-bird god, who is also Huitzilopochtli), told them: "Take your jewels and travel south till you come to a place where you will see an eagle perched on a cactus, eating a snake."

So the Aztec tribe began its pilgrimage, its forty years' wandering in the wilderness, like the Children of Israel, carrying their humming-bird god in a litter. From time to time the god spoke to them, directing them the way they should go.

[1] Alfonso Caso, *La religión de los Aztecas* (Mexico, 1936).

But the humming-bird god was a "left-handed humming-bird", which is perhaps as much as to say that he was also something else. In fact, he was the god of war; and, as such, he led the Aztecs through the wilderness. When they reached the lakes near Mexico, they sent out two messengers to look for the eagle sitting on a cactus and eating a snake. One of the messengers fell into the lake and was pulled down to the bottom, where he saw Tlaloc, the god of rain. Tlaloc told him that this was the place appointed; and they eventually found the eagle perched on a cactus with a snake in his beak, as had been foretold.

The name Mexico is a memorial to the humming-bird god Mexi, and Tenochtitlan (the name of the city which Cortés conquered) was called so as being the place of the fruit of the cactus, *tenoch*. "The City of Mexico (to tell the story in the words of Srta Martínez del Río) was once an island city. It was surrounded by lakes, and the Aztecs called it the 'Lady of the Lakes'. The lakes were encircled by a border of green, broad highways, which joined the city to the mainland."

On the lakes, canoes came and went continually, loaded with flowers and vegetables from the country round. In the middle rose the magnificent temple of the humming-bird. This temple was enclosed by a huge stone wall, surmounted by carved serpents. The temple of the war god was built on a squat pyramid. Around this pyramid was a court with floors so highly polished that the Spaniards thought it was made of silver. There the sacred dances were celebrated. Scattered round this pyramid were scores of smaller temples built to honour the less important gods. The Aztec people in their last epoch worshipped a countless number of gods. They even worshipped the gods of all the tribes they conquered, and for these gods they had a special temple built, called Coatlan, "the place of serpents". The temple of the humming-bird and all the adjoining temples were built of stone, profusely carved and painted in deep, rich colours. The houses of the city were of stone, each with its garden. The streets were half water and half solid ground, so that people could travel on foot or in a canoe.

Of the Aztec arts, everyone has read something: their stone work, their jewels of gold and silver; their cotton, woven and dyed; their work in feathers: the obsidian (or volcanic glass) which they cut and polished for ornaments and knives; their jade. They wrote (or, rather, drew) with ink made from burnt wood; they kept records in books, and made coloured maps. They knew how to measure time—to a quarter of a second, it is said; they kept calendars for the sun, moon and Venus; all their temples had observatories. They were religious (or superstitious), with a cruel irreligious piety, they had a high standard of conduct, great respect for old age, and they worshipped their dead in the belief that they had awakened to another life. Although, at the moment of the Spanish conquest, they had a polytheistic religion, with a multitude of personal gods with well-defined attributes, a belief in magic and occult forces played a great part among the less instructed. At the other end of the scale there was a philosophical school which held that the origin of all things came from a dual principle, masculine and feminine, which had engendered the gods, the world, and all mankind. One of the kings, Neza-hualcoyotl, who reigned in Texcoco, had reached the idea of belief in one god, invisible in the highest heaven: the first cause, and God above all gods.

The Aztecs have been condemned, from the very first, for their practice of human sacrifice. It was this custom that so roused the horror of the Spaniards: not merely the horror of the act, but the condition of the temples and the appalling smell. Bernal Díaz makes that quite clear. Yet the Aztecs have been by no means the only nation to indulge in human sacrifice. Something might be said of the Spaniards them-selves, on that account, and of the Holy Inquisition; though the human sacrifice which at various times has taken place in Spain cannot be compared with what was performed in the

Aztec Empire under Montezuma. Further, it should not be forgotten that Montezuma had some justification for the custom. It was a theological justification. Man (it was held) had been created by the sacrifices of the gods; man therefore owed the gods his own blood. His contribution, and collaboration, were indispensable; for the gods could not exist without being nourished, and their nourishment was a mystic substance in the blood of man. *Tantum religio...!*

I hope that what I have written here will never be read by T. A. Joyce! He had the gift of making the complex tribal history of ancient Mexico intelligible, and would be horrified at my attempts at simplification. In memory of his excellent sherry, and a journey we once made together to Madrid, I can only refer a reader to his *Mexican Archaeology* (1914), and to the illustrated edition of Prescott's *History of the Conquest of Mexico* for which he wrote an admirable introduction.

Chapter VII

CHRISTMAS IN MEXICO

A few days before Christmas I was invited to a *posada*—not an inn (as the word *posada* would have indicated in Spain), but a Christmas party in the Mexican style. Not to disappoint the folk-lorists and those interested in picturesque customs, I must say at once that it was not a popular demonstration, or a slum party, but a party given by the wife of an old Mexican friend. It was a late party, and began with hot drinks; while from numerous little tables you could help yourself to various kinds of nuts and biscuits, and also to little books of the words of old Spanish carols. The house was a pleasant and fairly modern flat; emphatically not one of those Mexican interiors of the age of Porfirio Díaz, described by Mr Stuart Chase, "filled with plush, gilt, crayon portraits of ferocious gentlemen with mustachios, and a black plaster sambo holding out a card tray". Both the flat and its owners belonged to a later age, and a younger generation.

There was a Christmas tree in one corner—a branch of Montezuma pine, I think—lighted with electric candles and decorated with the usual glass ornaments; but instead of holly and bunches of red berries there were great branches of flaming crimson *Poinsettias*; indeed the Mexican name for *Poinsettia* is Flower of Christmas Eve (*Flor de Noche Buena*). Meanwhile we were each given a little green, red or white candle to hold; green, white and red being the colours of the Mexican flag. There was a faint ceremony about the lighting. You did not just light your candle: the sacred fire had to be conveyed to you by someone who had already received it.

Then the guests were divided into two groups. One group represented pilgrims, and went out into the courtyard; in villages they go round with candles and images of Joseph and Mary, singing and looking for a lodging. I looked round for a *nacimiento*, a "crib"; the stable with the Holy Family; shepherds and shepherdesses singing and playing on musical instruments, the Three Kings with a fabulous procession of camels, the Angels of Peace and Good Will precariously seated on a cloud, the Star in the East with a real electric bulb, and a farmyard filled with enough animals to have stocked a cattle show, and irrigated by a Spanish waterwheel and real water. That was the sort of *nacimiento* I remembered in Madrid; but those on sale in the Mexican markets had been of a less complicated kind. They were not arranged for real water, but were interesting because the little figures were real Mexicans, and an ethnologist would no doubt have observed that Joseph's features were strongly Tarascan, and Mary a native of the Isthmus of Tehuantepec, while the shepherds and shepherdesses would have been composed of Nahuas, Mayas, Zapotecs, Otomíes, Totonacs and all the other races which go to make up the Indian part of Mexico to-day.

There may have been a *nacimiento* in the house, but I could not see it; and meanwhile someone was lighting my candle and finding my place in the book of words. Outside, the pilgrims began to sing to be let in; while inside, we sang back at them, and did not open the door until the last verse. Then, after another round of punch, the second part of the ceremony began: the *piñata*.

Why the *piñata* is called so, I have not been able to determine. The word seems to be Italian in origin: *pignatta*, a pot. A Mexican *piñata* is something made of pottery, or paper, filled with sweets and hung up so that it may be broken with a stick by someone blindfolded. It is not unknown in Spain, but comes at carnival, not at Christmas. On this occasion the *piñata* was a doll about 3 ft. high, dressed in "Spanish" clothes with a reminiscence of Goya, and a mantilla made of black, cut paper, which the lady of the house afterwards presented to me. The *piñata* was hanging from a hook out in the yard. One guest after another was blindfolded, turned round and round and then given a stick to hit at it, before it was pulled quickly up or down to keep it out of the way. At last, when the *piñata* was considerably damaged, a lucky hit broke it to pieces, in a shower of oranges, limes, nuts and chocolates.

Then came an excellent stand-up supper; but everything was extremely dignified and decorous—Mexicans are, if anything, more formal than Spaniards, and have at least as much stately Spanish grace—until (and it was the dramatic climax of the evening) there entered the Messenger.

The Messenger is not part of the usual ceremony of a *posada*. His appearance on this occasion was unexpected and unrehearsed; but it was as appropriate—and, as we found afterwards, as tragic—as the entrance of the Messenger in a Greek play. He brought news from Spain—news that thousands of Spanish and Spanish-speaking people had been expecting, but news which had been delayed for over two years. The Spanish people behind the rebel general's lines had risen (he said); there had been fighting between Franco's men and the foreign "volunteers" who had come to help him. Further, a number of rebel Spanish officers, sick of *Falange* and its ways, had gone over to the Government lines, taking with them the maps and plans for the rebel offensive to be delivered on Christmas Day. At that, the whole spirit of the party changed; it was the best possible good news that could possibly have reached a Christmas party; it really seemed the return of peace on earth to men of good will. We did not know then that the war was to be decided, not in Spain but in London; and that Italian intervention was less effective than Italian bluff.

Such spontaneous and outspoken sympathy for the Spanish Republic—for the "other Spain"—was not only encouraging;

it was very interesting. For my own part, long and intimate connection with Spain had made it impossible, from the very beginning, to take any other point of view; no one with my experience of the Spanish character could have failed to see through such conventional Spanish types as the rebel leaders. Yet this was not a Spanish party, nor was it a "left" party. It was a private gathering of Mexicans; and until the Spanish military revolt and foreign invasion of Spain had roused the horror and sympathy of all Mexicans of good will (who, after all, have suffered more than most people from military revolt and the degradations of war), a Mexican was not necessarily a friend of Spain any more than an Irish American is a friend of England. A few Spaniards were present on this occasion, and I myself (as someone said) was there as an "honorary Spaniard", in much the same way as the Japanese have been appointed "honorary Aryans". But the result of the entrance of the Messenger was a sudden outburst of sympathy. The whole spirit of the party changed: bottles of champagne appeared as if by a conjuring trick; someone handed round tots of real whisky; and though every member of the company retained perfect manners and almost perfect sobriety, the party grew extremely lively, and while an Asturian sang the wild songs of his dear native land, the rest of us sang again—in unison, or such unison as we could manage—the Spanish carols we had sung earlier in the evening.

Our hostess was the wife of a Mexican civil servant whom, twenty years before, I had met in Madrid. He was not so much a Latin American as a Gallic American, with the spirit of Montaigne and the humour of Anatole France. At our first meeting he had ragged me considerably about the authorship of that curious and fascinating production, *The Young Visiters*. In England we believed—we knew—that the author was a small girl; and that the manuscript had been shown to Barrie and published just as it stood. There had been, it was true, a case of much the same kind in America:

another small girl, from the backwoods of some remote state (it was said), had written an extraordinary book on the backs of dead leaves; and though the genuineness of this was vouched for and defended by no less a person than Sir Edward Grey, it was (to all English readers of *The Young Visiters*) a palpable fake. *The Young Visiters*, however, could be proved to be genuine from internal evidence. The unconscious snobbery of it all; Mr Salteena, the character who was "not quite the thing", the Earl of Clinchem, who, in arranging for the social education and "finishing" of Mr Salteena, remarked "You will mix with me for manners", a saying which, in a German edition, would have taken and received a whole page of footnotes. Further there was the somewhat unexpected Roman Catholic atmosphere, ". . . and they had two children, one of whom was called Ignatius. . . ." These things could not have been invented by Barrie, or any mature author: they were the genuine experiences of a Victorian English child, brought up as a Catholic and left a good deal with the servants. But my Mexican friend swept aside all these reasons with a wave of his hand; my arguments, he said, would convince no one but the converted; they were like the arguments of Catholic theologians or ingenious Jesuits. While there seemed to be good evidence that the American book had really been written on dead leaves by a small child, *The Young Visiters* was obviously written by Barrie. Its length, for instance; and its form. Everybody knew that the average English novel was as long as an Indian epic; but here was a short novel, of the length and form of a Barrie. There were other arguments which I have forgotten; but my Mexican friend (who even then, was already well known for his essays, his poems, and his editions of Spanish classics) used all the technique and resources of scholarship to prove that I was wrong. The name of the heroine, for instance: Ethel Montague. Montague. That name presupposed a knowledge of *Romeo and Juliet*, unlikely in a small child of the age imputed to the author of *The Young Visiters*. It was useless for me to declare that many English families must have known, or known of, people who called themselves Montague; the argument would only have been true if the heroine had been called Capulet. But it was no good. My arguments, once again—and there was an unforgettable twinkle, as he said it—were only convincing to the already converted. I went away with a memory of one of the most amusing discussions I ever had; and it was one of the great joys of my second visit to Mexico to be able to pick up our acquaintance where we had left it, and even more or less on the same plane that we had left it; the plane of ripe but frivolous scholarship.

On Christmas Eve I went to another *posada*. Our host on this occasion was in the Mexican Treasury, and lived in a delightful modern house, but one that was not at all large or pompous, in one of the numerous "colonies" or Hampsteads surrounding Mexico City. The main room was a large hall, with a staircase running up one side and leading to a gallery which went along the whole of one wall. There were quantities of English books—and books published in England, too; they evidently belonged to a man who was Anglophil in the truest and best possible sense, yet he had apparently been unknown to the British Legation, which seemed to have had little contact with any Mexicans except supporters of the old regime and dispossessed landowners who had been educated by English Jesuits.

A Cabinet Minister was present, or came about half-way through, and our host suggested that he might like to talk to me; for there were then, in Mexico, no British representatives or "relations" of any kind. I said that my "relations", the relations I was interested in, were purely cultural; I knew nothing about *oil*, and had nothing to do with it: but regretted any action (by the British Government) upsetting friendly relations with a country which interested me, and which I found to be full of friendly people. The Minister had meanwhile come up to us, and overheard what I was saying. "Oil need not blacken our relations!" he said. "Try some of our host's Armagnac." I saw him again and had a long conversation, a few days afterwards.

The *posada* was on the same general plan as the other one. As the night was mild, we walked round the garden in procession, singing carols, with lighted Christmas-tree candles in our hands. There was, of course, a *piñata*; this time it was in the shape of a donkey and hung from the branch of a tree. They insisted that I should be the first to hit at it, and all blindfolded as I was, I nearly brained my host with the walking stick. After supper, there was dancing. Beside the usual dances there were comic dance turns, for men only; one ludicrous *pas seul* was executed by a former rector of the University of Madrid, a grave and philosophical pupil of Ortega y Gasset. There was also a comic dance with some particular object, each solo turn of which ended by presenting the object unexpectedly to another. Then there was a new American dance, a "follow-my-leader", in which everyone joined, and had to do exactly what was done by the person in front. This ended by going up the flight of stairs which ran up one long wall of the room, and turning round in the gallery along the shorter wall. It looked curiously attractive, with the lights turned down, and only the winking bulbs on the Christmas tree; for, on the tree, the lights came and went as they do in a comic film I saw on the ship, in which some people in a Paris flat, having no money for the electric slot meter, connected their lights with the illuminated sign outside. Unfortunately it was of the kind that winked. An attractive thing about the party was that everyone was young—at least there was no one very old; and that all the women were distinctly good-looking, and married. I left earlier than most, but it was after four when I got back to the hotel.

Chapter VIII

EXCURSION WITH EMMA

It was about this time that an excursion was arranged to Puebla and Cholula; and this was the occasion on which Emma came too.

Emma is a person of uncertain age—uncertain to me, at any rate; at that time she could hardly have achieved double figures. I first met her at a tea party. We were saying good-bye, and she emerged from another room, looking like a Mexican Alice-in-Wonderland. Her next appearance was on this two-day excursion, arranged by her father to show one of the seven Spaniards and myself some of the seven wonders of Mexico: Tlaxcala, Ocotlán, Huejotzingo, Cholula, Tonant-zintla, Acatepec, and Puebla. Emma, of course, had been there before—to some of them, at any rate; and during some parts of the journey I think she dozed a little in the back of the car. I suppose I did too, sometimes; though on a bright December morning in Mexico, even a sleepy person like myself was able to keep awake. Yet Emma was the most alert and self-possessed of anyone. She had an exquisite pronunciation for the Aztec names of the places we passed, and was very proud of the few words she knew of Náhuatl, the modern Aztec language. She was quite ready to light and start a cigarette for her father when she sat beside him driving; and when she sat in the back, she knew exactly when to look out, and where. She was glad to get out, when the car stopped, but not very anxious to go into the churches; the business of balancing a little square handkerchief on her head, so that she should not be, theologically speaking, naked, seemed to her mere silliness. At lunch in Puebla, she ordered the nicest peppery dish of any of us, but was distinctly critical of a lemon ice, seeing that the town has an ice-cream factory, a *fábrica de helados*, of its own. Her ambition just then, I think, was to be herself the owner of a *fábrica de helados*; but I remembered afterwards, with my usual *esprit d'escalier*, that I had not told her that my own home town in England, though it has no factory for ice-cream, certainly manufactures jam and marmalade—has, in fact, *una fábrica de mermeladas*. Not that Emma was greedy. On the contrary, it was rather difficult to make her eat anything at all.

We passed the remains of Lake Texcoco, on its other side, opposite the road going to Teotihuacán. Texcoco is a problem. It is the last remaining lake—except the canals at Xochimilco—of those which practically surrounded Mexico City at the time of the conquest, and it is salt. Drainage has left a salt soil—not common salt, but a mixture of salts in which nothing will grow. (It consists chiefly of sodium carbonate, with small quantities of bicarbonate, common salt and sodium sulphate, and traces of calcium chloride and calcium carbonate.) The rains leave puddles: but they soon dry up, and turn to dust—a fine, penetrating, alkaline dust mixed with small sharp-edged crystals. This dust is dangerous to people living near, and it is dangerous when it blows into Mexico City. The problem is to find some plant which could be grown there first, to bind the soil and prepare it for something useful. The only things that grow wild are *romeritos* (*Suaeda* and *Dondia*) and a few grasses.

Leaving Lake Texcoco, the road runs past the quarry of pink *tezontle*, the stone of which the characteristic colonial houses in Mexico were built, up into the mountains: a fine mountain road and a national park, of pine woods with tall crimson salvias growing by the roadside; past Río Frío, a Wild-West-looking settlement in a hollow at the top of the range, which has been nibbling at the pine woods for so long that, just there, they have receded almost to the hill-tops. The declaration of the whole district as a national park and the introduction of stringent forestry laws has at last, it seems, put an end to the nibbling.

Then down to Tlaxcala, the city of the chief allies of Cortés, with a plaza embowered in big trees, and dazzling white buildings against an intense blue sky. A heavily built sixteenth-century arcaded town hall; a curious piece of decoration, in Renaissance style, but carried out by Indians; a *cenefa*, over a window, which I photographed for our host, and a church with flashing coloured tiles on the tower and dome, and sonnets hanging in the porch. One of them runs as follows; it is musical, if nothing else.

> Como el arroyo puro y cristalino,
> que por doquier que va brotan las flores,
> y forman un mosaico de colores
> las riberas de todo su camino:
> Así Jesús purísimo y divino,
> fuente de bendición, fuente de amores,
> esparce por doquiera sus labores,
> mejorando del hombre su destino.
> Por eso el pecador, que atribulado
> invoca la piedad del sacramento
> se cura de la lepra del pecado.
> Se le vuelve la dicha y el contento,
> y a la región eterna es elevado
> para habitar allá en el firmamento.

A Spanish friend has capped this sonnet with an inscription on the church door at San Miguel de Allende, in the State of Guanajuato:

La puntualidad es virtud de santos, cortesía de reyes, deber de caballeros, necesidad de hombres de negocios y costumbre de hombres de juicio.

Punctuality is the virtue of Saints, the courtesy of kings, the duty of gentlemen, the need of men of business and the custom of men of sound judgment.

From Tlaxcala, up a hill to the incredibly Churrigueresque church of Ocotlán. It has a tiled façade and dome, and a pair of curiously beautiful towers wider at the top than at the bottom. The interior was partially modernized in the nine-teenth century (like the interior of so many Mexican churches); but the chancel and transepts were most fortunately left as they were, and the Churrigueresque retablos glow much as they did when the Indian carver finished them. Both these and the *camarín*, the private chamber of the miraculous Virgin of Ocotlán, have appropriately been compared to an enchanted grotto.

We went back a few miles, joined the main road to Puebla, and stopped for a little at the magnificent sixteenth-century monastery at Huejotzingo. A broad flight of nine or ten steps leads through three round arches into a great court full of old trees and a large church; the apse is built like a fortress, necessary in this outpost of empire so soon after the conquest. The district became a great place for fruit trees, apple, pear and plum, imported originally from Europe. Earlier in the day we had passed some of the few, old and venerable Spanish olive trees which remain: there are said to be some 240 left in the country, planted in the sixteenth and seventeenth centuries; but they have not been replaced. Olive takes too long before it will bear, and Mexican landowners liked quicker returns.

I have forgotten which was the monastery, rather like Huejotzingo, with a double-arched doorway leading into a tree-lined court. I remember it chiefly for the enormous turkey strutting about the churchyard but refusing to pose so that a photograph would show him at his best. Turkeys are said to have first been found in Mexico. Someone has written a book on what Europe is supposed to owe to Spanish civilization; but (so far as I remember) he says nothing about the admirable things to eat, which the *conquistadores* (the least greedy of men, one would have thought) found in Mexico and brought back to Europe: turkeys, pineapples, chocolate. Mexican Spanish has two pleasant words for turkey: *guajolote* (for the he) and *pípila* (for the she), but such *Aztequismos*, or Aztecisms, are an amusing subject which must come later.

And so, leaving Cholula for the next day, we ran into Puebla. The first impressions were good: a clean, geometrical town—most Mexican towns are clean and geometrical—with straight streets cutting one another at right-angles, for such were the orders of the Spanish Government at home; full of nobly designed colonial houses with beautiful and surprising façades, pleasant squares planted with large trees and carefully tended flowers, and baroque churches covered with gleaming coloured tiles. But I was appalled at the religiosity of the place: tracts thrust into your hands, individuals standing at the church doors to take a collection even before you could look in to see whether the interior was worth looking at, subversive posters, and the motto of the *Cristeros* —the "Christ's men"—bloodiest and most barbarous of all Mexican revolutionaries, who chiefly distinguished themselves by blowing up bridges and wrecking trains to the greater glory of God. *¡Viva Cristo Rey!* Further, the Christian festival of peace, Christmas, seemed to be of no account in this home of the new Christianity; so far as one could see, there were no preparations whatever for the celebration of a festival; no sign of *nacimientos* in the churches, nor anything like that performance mentioned by Madame Calderón de la Barca: a Christmas entertainment in the old theatre to which she was advised not to go, because there would be men there smoking and drinking brandy! It is to be feared that there is less of poetry than of business in modern Mexican Catholicism. The duty of a Catholic is to save his own soul, to turn out the Government and restore their property to the big landlords and the Church.

In Puebla, there were no signs of the religious persecution about which pious people in England and the United States tell you with shocked voices. The idea of persecution of the Church in Mexico seems to have arisen from the ill-judged activities of Garrido Canabal, ex-Governor of "godless" Tabasco, a dictator of a curious type, who occupied his shirted followers in baiting priests as if they were Jews. This

Puebla: Tiled House

Puebla: Casa de Alfeñique

was a splendid opportunity for propaganda: now at last the Church could complain of something like real persecution. Finally the Government sent the picturesque priest-baiter an aeroplane, with orders to get into it, and not show his face in Mexico again. But the harm was done; and much as the present rulers of Mexico may loathe and distrust the Catholic Church, they dread it too much to offend it or oppose it openly.

But if Puebla is the most beautiful of all Mexican cities, its beauty does not depend on the churches so much as on the private houses. Churches adorned with Puebla tiles are certainly wonderful, both in the town and in the country round. We drove out to Acatepec and Tonantzintla: a perfectly flat plain with nothing there except a cactus or two, a background of volcanoes, and these incredible baroque churches, shimmering with coloured tiles in the afternoon sun. Popocatépetl and Iztaccíhuatl lay to the west, Malinche to the north-east; while far away, seventy miles or so in a due easterly direction, was the towering snowy peak of Orizaba. But next morning, when we continued our exploration of Puebla, we found that not only the churches were tiled, but many of the splendid colonial houses as well. There is no street in the centre of Puebla in which one cannot find beautiful and original examples of Spanish colonial houses. The show place is the House of Icing-Sugar, *Casa de Alfeñique*; but there is an even better one in the same street and so many others in different parts of the town, that most visitors (and most guide-books) take them for granted and pay no attention to them. There is the Hotel Arronte, for instance; the Dolls' House, *Casa de las Muñecas*; and dozens more, with splendidly proportioned façades, and endless variations in what seem to be the two main characteristics of domestic architecture in Puebla: the use of coloured tiles and the practice of carrying the jambs of the windows right up to the cornice.

The House of Icing-Sugar must have belonged to a typical clerical family. The rather oppressive "period" rooms bristle with notices telling you not to do things. There are no books, beyond one devotional one which you are not allowed to touch or see the title-page; no pictures, except the grim portraits of avaricious ecclesiastics. It is all curiously unpleasant, as a museum, and the period rooms are nothing out of the ordinary. The best part of it is the little pre-colombian (Toltec and Aztec) museum on the ground floor. Out again to the Market, which has curious architectural hoods to cover the stalls; and to an amusing blue church, with the early sun slanting on the plaster walls. It would have pleased Ronald Firbank, who in one of his novels describes a church called the "Blue Jesus".

Then we saw the stone marking the spot where a good Spanish poet was killed in a quarrel: Gutierre de Cetina, famous for his sonnets and for a madrigal (*Ojos claros, serenos*) which is in every anthology of Spanish verse. I once found the original music for it in a manuscript in the library of the Duke of Medinaceli, arranged as a madrigal for four voices; and it was also printed as a solo, with an accompaniment for a Spanish lute. Cetina and a friend went out for a walk one night before turning in; unfortunately they took their guitars with them instead of their swords. They were set upon by hired assassins and murdered where they stood. The ruffians were not after the poet, but his friend; and not knowing which was which, they thought it safer to make an end of both.

Our last visit in Puebla was to the Palafox Library which has the books accessible to the public on splendid baroque shelves, and a most obliging staff, ready to give the inquiring visitor every help. We did not visit the much-advertised "secret" convent, which was said to have gone on as a convent, eluding the watchfulness of the Government, ever since the Constitution of 1917 made such puerilities illegal. It is now a museum of ecclesiastical art.

Puebla seems to have been founded directly by the *conquistadores*. It is doubtful whether there was even a village there before; and if it were not for the bizarre beauty of the baroque style when it runs to coloured tiles, there would have been no justification whatever for building so many churches. At Cholula, however, there was a justification. Cholula had been a great centre of pagan worship; the place was full of pyramids, on the top of which were those "stinking temples" (as the Spaniards called them); and there religious superstition demanded not only perpetual human sacrifice, but that neither temples nor priests should ever be washed. Down by the coast, Cortés persuaded the fat cacique of Zempoalla to have his priests washed, especially their heads; but at Cholula he could do nothing of the kind, for he and all his men were in danger of being massacred. They only escaped by massacring a good number of their enemies first; and, after the conquest of Mexico, they set to work to build a church on the site of every pagan pyramid they could find. In Cholula they found 365 of them; but nevertheless the churches were built and are there to this day, though most of the inhabitants have migrated to Puebla, leaving only about 8000—mainly Indians—to the enjoyment of the 365 churches.

The traditions of Cholula go back to the Toltec story of the Flood. The Flood came to an end and the earth was dry again. Not only were a man and a woman saved, but seven giants who had taken refuge in a cave on the top of the Mountain of Tlaloc. When the waters subsided, the giants left their cave, and coming down on the beautiful plains of Cholula, "they ran and gambolled, happy to be alive". They built a temple to the god Tlaloc, because they owed him their lives; but it was looked on by the other gods as a tower of Babel, and the builders were destroyed, though not the pyramid, which is there to this day, with the usual church on the top of it. The church has been too drastically restored in modern times to have much interest; but out on the terrace the views are superb. In front, the snowy caps of Popo and Izta, not much more than twenty miles away; and at the back, framed, on that bright December morning, by a leafless tree with large, orange flowers, another snow-mountain, Malinche.

This was as near as the Aztecs could get to pronouncing Doña Marina (as the Spaniards called her), the Aztec girl, speaking both Aztec and Maya, presented to Cortés by the Cacique of Tabasco. Cortés made her his interpreter (his "tongue") and then his mistress, and she accompanied him on all his greatest undertakings. It was Doña Marina, more than anyone else, who discovered the plot which was being prepared at Cholula to put Cortés and all his men safely out of the way; and though, for form's sake, he married her off to one of his men, he was never seen anywhere without her, and himself became known to the Indians as *Malintzin*, "owner of Malintzi". But to her own people, of course, Doña Marina was a traitress; without her Cortés would never have got to Mexico at all. So in popular imagination she became the *Llorona*, the "weeping one", the white phantom, the lost soul that never rests or ceases lamenting all through the dark night, for having betrayed her country to the Spaniards. "Denied the beneficent peace of the tomb, when she reached the threshold of eternity an angel appeared to her, and showed her a vision of the desolation brought on her country by the Spanish conquerors. She was condemned to suffer for three centuries. During the day the turbid waters of Texcoco should be her tomb, and during the night she should wander through the conquered city, breathing out mournful groans which only ceased when the bird of morning was heard in the tree-tops announcing the new day." The curse was fulfilled, and after three centuries had passed she was allowed to return to her tomb. But she cannot have stayed there. I seem to see her on a misty morning, haunting the rocky cactus slopes of her mountain, calling (in three languages) a warning to all linguists to think before they speak.

The pyramid of Cholula is covered now with trees and wild flowers; it would be hard to say which months had more blossom, December or August. There is an old Spanish road up it, with none of those terrifying, barbaric flights of steps, such as face you at Teotihuacán; for the Cholula Pyramid, though it goes back to the time of the Toltecs, has not been restored as an archaeological monument. Excavations have been made; tunnels have been driven through this mound as through others; but they are only of interest to professed archaeologists. Nothing that I saw, then or afterwards, in the whole of Mexico, has left a stronger or more lasting impression than the landscape of fields and gardens, tiled domes and snow-capped volcanoes seen from the flowery pyramid of Cholula.

Yet Cholula is not (as Herr Baedeker used to say) suitable for a prolonged stay. Those writers who judge the prosperity of a Mexican town by the number of its churches, would no doubt give Cholula full marks. Some of its churches are certainly remarkable buildings; the Capilla de los Reyes has nine aisles and little domes budding out all over the roof, like the cathedral at Córdoba in Spain. But there is no escaping the fact that Cholula has no hotel or restaurant, or even a café; so after some pleasantly peppery sandwiches put together for us by Emma and her father at a small *tienda de abarrotes*, or colonial warehouse, we crossed the mountains once more on a lovely afternoon's journey back to Mexico City.

The last excursion I made before hurrying back to England was to Cuernavaca and Taxco. It was made with two friends, one English and the other American: comparatively old hands in Mexico, yet without either the "intense though often suppressed irritation", or "that bitter hopelessness that comes over people who know Mexico well" which D. H. Lawrence found in Mexico fifteen years ago.

Up to a 10,000 ft. pass, through dense woods of oak, chestnut, pine and juniper. Then across a lonely, desolate moor of peat and bog, and down into a subtropical country on the Pacific slope, through pines, arbutus and oaks; with maidenhair and other ferns, wild dahlias (at least, in August, when I went again); scarlet salvias and blue lupins; and the road, still dominated, on the lower slopes, by the snowy top of

Popo. Then on to Taxco by a road on the edge of a fearsome precipice, a road which even the best driver in Mexico might find awkward, if the second-best driver came tearing down on the inside of a curve.

Taxco was the nearest to a Spanish town which I had yet seen in Mexico. It is certainly picturesque; and now that the large new hotel has been perched on the top of the hill over the silver mine, the Government has decreed that no new houses are to be built in the town so as to spoil it. If only this had been done in Toledo! If only a hundred years ago the whole of England had been put under a glass case! As it is, Taxco is extremely decorative: with something of Segovia and something of Granada, not like either, yet still very Spanish; and it has a market in which (the authorities say) the *Otomí* Indian embroideries, and other wares, are genuine.

Cuernavaca—the name has nothing to do with a "horn" or a "cow", but was the nearest Cortés and his friends could get to the Aztec word—Cuernavaca is distinctly attractive, though some people darkly hint that it is getting too like Hollywood. There is a palace of Cortés, with a wonderful view of Popo and a gallery decorated with amusing frescoes by Diego Rivera making fun of the *conquistadores* in their leader's own house. (Even a *conquistador*, sleeping under a little image of the B.V.M., may sometimes have gone to bed drunk, or accompanied by a brown companion.)

The best thing in Cuernavaca is the Borda Garden. In the eighteenth century a Monsieur Bordes made a fortune out of the silver mine at Taxco. Having blown a considerable portion of it in building Taxco Cathedral, he then lost the remainder and had to begin all over again. He made another fortune, and this time—perhaps in the meanwhile he had been reading *Candide*—he put it into a garden, which is still one of the most beautiful gardens of its kind anywhere, full of mangoes and fig-trees, with a grove of pomegranates, and oranges and lemons, aguacate, zapote, chirimoyas and bananas. The house is now a good restaurant, though the garden is neglected; yet

Tarascan Indian dug-out (*Lake of Pátzcuaro*)

Taxco: On the roof of the Cathedral

it is a superb ruin, in the style of the Generalife at Granada. There is a large swimming pool, the most memorable thing in the garden, where the poor Empress, "Mama" Carlota, used to bathe with her maids of honour on warm evenings—in bathing costumes designed by Winterhalter? A crinoline could hardly have got into those bathing cabins.

The last day in Mexico was a nightmare. After a very pleasant lunch with the editor of a newspaper—and he asked me to his home, not to a restaurant, so that I had the pleasure of meeting his family—I was condemned that evening to be interviewed. I carefully prepared my impromptu, wrote it down, had it vetted by a Spanish friend, and duly turned up at the office, where, for five minutes I wandered about like a lost soul (or like Malinche herself) trying to find the man who was expecting me. Then alas, my passport photograph was not thought good enough, and a staff photographer was summoned, provided with a flashlight. He produced a still more passport-looking photograph, I handed in my interview, and fled. Next morning I caught the "City of Mexico", a through train to St Louis, Mo., which goes once a week, but not every week. It is a long journey northwards across Mexico; and almost from the first the sun deserted us. But American sleeping-cars are far in advance of anything produced in Europe, and it was not without pleasure and recognition that I found myself once more in a country of northern frosts, northern mists and good coffee.

Chapter IX

SECOND ARRIVAL

I had left Mexico on December 30th and was back again on April 6th. In that short time the whole outlook of the Spanish-speaking world had changed. By strokes of pens in London and Paris, formal recognition had been given to the *Caudillo* in Spain; and that meant that all Spaniards not in possession of Franco passports were outcasts, people who might not travel freely where they would, but were likely to be stopped and turned back as undesirable aliens, unless they had special permission to enter a country and special guarantees from people living in that country. This was only one more instance of the curious discrimination which, from the beginning of General Franco's rebellion and the German-Italian invasion of Spain, had been made against the legitimate republican government. As long as the war lasted, illegal, rebel "passports" had been winked at in all foreign countries; while rebel emissaries, propagandists and spies had come and gone freely in Europe and America. But the moment the *Generalísimo* received official recognition from the Powers, the legal republican passports were no longer accepted. The only exceptions were those governments in America which still recognized the Republic, and these included Mexico and the United States.

My first visit to Mexico had been mainly, and before everything else, a visit to a former Spanish colleague who had been a teacher in my University; and I had then undertaken to bring out to Mexico a member of his family who had been working in Paris. It was a moral obligation—the greatest moral obligation which has ever been laid upon me—to keep my word, in spite of Members of Parliament and Government officials and the indecent haste of my own misguided country to recognize a totalitarian Spanish general. "He may not be a great General", one of the London Sunday papers had written, "he may not be a great Statesman. But he is a,great Catholic, and a great gentleman; and he has a golf handicap." I began to calculate what my own handicap was in these difficult circumstances, if I were to convey a Spanish refugee from Europe to America.

To begin with, a British ship was impossible, either to New York, Havana or Jamaica; the companies could not accept a Spanish refugee without a "valid" passport, nor could any French line via New York or direct to Veracruz. The only direct line from England to Mexico was German; and that, of course, was out of the question for both of us, apart from the fact that these ships put into Franco-Spanish ports, where my refugee might have been seized and handed over to the Spanish authorities on shore, to be dealt with after various months of imprisonment, or else condemned to the nameless hardships of a concentration camp. There remained the Dutch and Norwegian freighters which took a few passengers from Europe to Mexican ports, and the United States Lines from Havre and Southampton to New York, and New York to Veracruz. I decided to trust the United States (which had not yet recognized General Franco); and with the very great help and friendliness of a certain agency in London, I managed it. Opposition came from a somewhat Nazi clerk in a certain Paris office; but it was eventually overcome through the efforts of a friend in New York, who took the matter up with the head office of the Line. For the voyage from New York to Veracruz, a doubt seemed at one time to arise in the mind of an official of Cuban extraction; but that, too, was overcome, and both voyages passed without incident and without great worry or anxiety to my companion. We were seen off at Southampton by friends from Cambridge; met in

New York, cared for, helped and seen off with that kind of efficient, thoughtful, American hospitality, which foresees everything and is ready for every emergency. I was glad that we had trusted the United States; and grateful, too, to a small deputation of undergraduates in England—the deputation included an American member of one of the women's colleges —who had come to see me one afternoon (when I was in bed with incipient influenza), and proposed a number of useful and practical suggestions.

So at last we arrived at Veracruz, and our journey ended in a sort of apotheosis, which would have appealed to students of Spanish mysticism: for, on the shores of the "True Cross", I left my companion folded in the arms of Jesús (the Christian name of a Spanish friend). Then, while he satisfied the authorities of "migration" on that blissful shore, by paying— in the manner traditional in Veracruz—a little more than had been expected, I was carried off to lunch by a Mexican acquaintance, to be introduced to the sauce called *a la Vera-cruzana*, and to hear the opinions of a Mexican on the Mexican writings of D. H. Lawrence.

Mornings in Mexico. That was not merely a pleasant, alliterative title. The mornings in Mexico are of peculiar beauty, particularly on the high plateau. There is a faint autumn feeling in the air, like a September morning in New York. The pale blue sky is bathed in a soft, surprised morning light, which lasts even when clouds begin to rise as the morning wears on; until, in the afternoons of the rainy season, they become black and heavy and eventually come down in torrents, and the day ends in a cool, spring evening. Lawrence was exquisitely sensitive to the beauty of the Mexican morning, and described it in a language which my host described as rhythmical, musical and full of mystery. His writings on Mexico are full of fine observation, surprises and delicate emotions. He had an original understanding for the primitive, and his descriptions are among the finest that have been made of Mexican landscape and Mexican man.

A mystical sense of the primitive. Lawrence understood this very clearly, because he had in himself—ultra-civilized as he felt—a vocation for the primitive something like that of Rousseau; a passion for nature and its mysterious processes, and a longing to get back to it, and wash his mind clean of the complications of western civilization. "Endless little details, words, attitudes, helped your great English poet to understand our primitive sensibility; to enjoy it, and sometimes even to invent it for himself."

Lawrence's Mexican landscape was finely drawn, simple and strong. His personality was made up of three or four main themes, which are always recurring in his pages; and his preoccupation with landscape was less than his passion for human life. In Lawrence, a Mexican reader finds the purity, greatness and nobility of the animal side of man's nature shown in its clearest manifestations. Man, with the imperious demands of his bodily necessities, the call of the "dark blood", the cry of the flesh, youth in its urge to perpetuate itself; Lawrence harmonized these things in many different forms and created symphonies of them. Of course, the clearly expressed intention of all this caused some readers discomfort; while others occasionally caught a glimpse of something very different: the Protestant Pastor and the Catechist, a side of him which pleased them less. In the end, it is his treatment of landscape which most holds the attention of the Mexican reader—Lake Chapala in *The Plumed Serpent*, and Oaxaca in *Mornings in Mexico*. He approached the primitive (my host thought) without sentimentalism and with nothing of the puerile admiration of the tourist. He lived close to the primitive, the elemental, the uncontaminated; and his writings have caught many of the peculiar qualities of the Mexican landscape and the Mexican character.

The varying moods of like and dislike for Mexico, which go to make a very real person of Kate in *The Plumed Serpent*, were partly Lawrence's own and partly those of Mrs Lawrence; for she loathed Mexico, and had been heard by Mexican witnesses roundly abusing it. The two sides of Kate are practically Lawrence and his wife; Lawrence trying hard to understand, thinking and feeling more deeply into the soul of Mexico than any other English writer, while Frida Lawrence was always unhappy and often bad-tempered. Lawrence was apt to say hard things about Mexico, and his opinions were sometimes violently contradictory; his intuition momentarily failed him when he took the side of "mixtifications" about occult forces and leaders of peoples. So the theme of restoring the religion of Quetzalcoatl is considered by Mexicans to be rather childish; while the Nazis (my friend informed me) have even claimed Lawrence as one of themselves. What, he asked, was really thought of Lawrence, now, in England? Lawrence was very English, surely, in his obsession with the view that morality meant respectability, and that the basis of respectability was the position one took on the question of sex? Had he not declared that the older civilizations—including the older Mexican civilizations—adopted a healthier attitude, and one that was less inhuman? Ideal love and prostitution, he declared, were only two ways of degrading the sexual act.

"Lawrence always seems to have been unhappy", I began, "in whatever society he found himself...." "Yes, that's it. And he tried to rediscover his lost social basis in his relations with women. Still (he continued), Lawrence is the most penetrating and profound modern writer who has visited Mexico, while it is probably through him that other English writers have done so," and he named Aldous Huxley, Rose Macaulay and Bernard Shaw.

A thing I had not bargained for at Veracruz was the number of people who travel at Easter. We had arrived on the Thursday before; and it was as hopeless trying to get in anywhere, as it would have been at Blackpool, Brighton or Bognor Regis. People from Veracruz go up to Mexico City, while people from Mexico City come down to Veracruz, with the result that there was not a room to be had; and rather than risk the complications of going to the house of the porter who looked after the luggage (he lived rather far out, and had already a German in his one spare room), I went to the hotel where the Air-line office is, and took a bed in a large room with nine single beds and two double ones. My destination was Mérida, in Yucatán; but there was no seat in the plane until Saturday. So I made a reservation for that day, and engaged a single bed for two nights. The hotel had a delightful two-storeyed colonial patio, covered with *Bougainvillea, Limonaria,* and a screaming, scarlet *Hibiscus* with a long pistil. The room I slept in was a kind of lounge, which was to be made later into a restaurant. I secured a corner bed by a window, and went to bed early. I saw that my next-bed neighbour looked like an Aztec mask. A local cinema was advertising a film called *No se duerma, profesor!* and I did not sleep very much.

There had been a strong north wind all day; and some time after midnight it began to rain tropically. The air grew suddenly cooler, then gradually warm again. Next morning the rain continued, and the temperature steadily dropped all day. About half-past three the patio became too chilly to sit in, while the force of the wind, and the amount of dust, made walking too unpleasant to be worth while. After coffee in the plaza—and Veracruz is one of the few places in Mexico where it is possible to sit and drink coffee out of doors—I had to sit in the lounge of the hotel in an overcoat and a hat; the north wind tore through every crack and cranny. These tropics!

The proprietors (two brothers), and the wife of one of them, were sad, but friendly. Among the illustrated papers for sale in a glass case in the hotel office was an alphabetical list of Mexican plants under their Spanish and Mexican names, with the scientific names and families and chief places of distribution in Mexico. I jumped at it (though it cost 10 Mexican dollars), and that broke any ice there might have been between me and the management. Changing travellers' cheques and business with the Air-line office also helped; and then one of the brothers showed me round the flowers in the patio. The names he gave were difficult to remember, let alone to identify. *Clavel*, for instance, usually means a pink or a carnation; but his *clavel de España* was certainly not a pink or a carnation. (It may have been *Cryptostegia*.) Again his *clavel de oro* was probably a *Turnera*. His *tulipán* and *tulipán doble*, were not tulips, but *Hibiscus*; his *limonaria*, a sweet, white-flowering shrub (which, like other things he had, only smelt at night). It seemed to be *Murraya*; and *Lluvia de oro* (golden rain). a low bush with golden spotted leaves, was—according to my new dictionary—*Tecoma*. The proprietor was one of those wise men, who, when the world goes wrong, fall back on cultivating a garden.

The din of Veracruz was appalling. What with mechanically propelled vehicles and mechanically produced music, there was no peace to be had anywhere. Shunting engines never moved without a shriek like a transatlantic liner starting for another continent; while the train which ran past the hotel to the bathing place had a steam whistle suitable for scaring elephants. It used to be said that the train which ran along the coast from Málaga had engines designed for the Belgian Congo and provided with whistles which would clear even an elephant off the line. But there are no elephants in America; and the last mammoth (though its flesh, when found, was still fresh and uncorrupted like that of a virgin martyr), died in America several centuries ago.

Chapter X

REFLECTIONS IN MÉRIDA

The aeroplane was timed to leave at 9 from Tejerías, the airport of Veracruz, about ten miles away. It got off pretty punctually, stopping at many tropical-looking places on the way; and as it was a dull morning and inclined to rain—a perfect morning, one of the passengers described it—there were no tropical discomforts. Minatitlán, the centre of an oil district, recently taken over by the Government; Villahermosa, chief town of "godless Tabasco"; Ciudad del Carmen, on an island in the remotest corner of the Bay of Campeche—an attractive-looking place, with a lagoon behind it, once occupied by British cutters of log-wood who seem eventually to have migrated to British Honduras; and, lastly, Campeche itself, a port on the Bay. The first three were airports, far from anything except thatched cottages—the type of thatched cottage that seems to be peculiar to these parts. But Ciudad del Carmen looked as if it might be a pleasant place, while Campeche, full of weather-beaten, pink and yellow houses and crumbling churches, seemed distinctly promising. It would be agreeable, I thought, to fly over one morning from Mérida, if only one could get a place on the plane going back. It could certainly have been done, and it is one of the things I shall always regret; indeed my chief sorrow in life is for the things I have left undone when travelling. The difficulty I found, afterwards, was to be sure of getting a place in the plane; and the afternoon train (which started back soon afterwards) took between five and six hours, whilst the morning train showed a puzzling time-table of nine hours and three-quarters.

The whole journey from Veracruz to Mérida was no longer than that from San Antonio to Mexico City; but it was more tiring, owing to the bumpy landings. I had wired to the only hotel I knew of in Mérida, and was met at the airport by the proprietor himself; but being very deaf after the plane, it was some time before I could make out who he was. I thought he might be a local government official to whom I had a letter of introduction; and was only reassured when we stopped at the hotel, and I was allotted a magnificently shabby suite, in a decaying colonial mansion, with two pleasant boys to look after me.

It was half-past three, and definitely within the tropics. The only thing to do was to take a siesta, and then a shower. After that, Mérida appeared as a perfect old Spanish town: clean, straight streets, at right angles, and all known by numbers— the odd numbers at right angles to the even. The chief impression of Spain came from the magnificent iron *rejas* over the windows. A Spanish friend, now in Mexico, once made a comparative study of the *rejas* in various parts of Southern Spain, and described the various types. Nearly all of them were to be seen here in Mérida: the iron grating unsupported, the grating supported by a ledge, and lastly the ledge becoming a step and supporting the *reja* from the ground.

The tradition of Spain in Mexico is more obvious in architecture than in anything else. There are ways of putting up a humble kind of building, and ways of setting to work to do any kind of job, that seem to me far more "Spanish" than anything in the Mexican character. The great paladin of "Spanishness" in Mexico is Sr Vasconcelos; but he, who might have become a Mexican Unamuno, has been soured and embittered by not being elected president, and then by having found it convenient to live in the one country which he most detests—the United States. From being a good writer and a considerable philosopher he seems to have drifted into the position of a pseudo-philosophic pseudo-historian, whose writings only serve as a quarry or ammunition dump for subversive Mexican newspapers and clerical propagandists.

Mérida: Iron rejas (supported on ledges)

Mérida: Curved reja (supported on step)

Mexicans of pure Spanish descent—the manager of the Mérida hotel, for instance—do not seem to me to "think Spanish". When they think at all, they are likely to think American. Otherwise they will probably think Jesuit; for a large number of them have been to school at Beaumont, or Stonyhurst, or the equivalent of these institutions in other European countries. They are of the landowning class, now rapidly being dispossessed—not gradually, by taxation, as in England, but suddenly and roughly, by expropriation; pillars of the Catholic Church, and inclined to look tolerantly on Fascism, or what they believe Fascism implies and the benefits which they fondly imagine it will bring. They praise the tradition of Spain because it is a Catholic tradition. Yet I should say that there was nothing Spanish about them now except their language; nor any connections or sympathies with any people in Spain, except a vague, unthinking notion that "Franco must be all right, because he is a Catholic and a gentleman". If they only knew it, one of the foundations of General Franco's policy, as originally laid down by his official spokesmen, was the expropriation of the large landowners.

Catholic writers, especially English Catholic writers and those who know little of America and nothing of Spain, are apt to exaggerate the importance of the Spanish tradition in Mexico. "The traditions of Spain (they say) are still deep in the Mexican character, and it is only by developing them that the country will ever grow happy." This seems like an attempt to pave the way for the restoration of the Spanish Empire in America, under the far-seeing, clement and cultured rule of Generalísimo Franco; it is a proposition of doubtful validity based on premises which are false. Mexico certainly inherited from Spain its architecture, its local government, and the blessings of the Catholic Church; but it is quite untrue to say that "the Mexicans, though they may sometimes *feel* like Aztecs...*think* like Spaniards". Those who think at all think like Americans, and feel (I should say) according to the amount of Indian blood they have in their veins. One thing that none of them do is to think or feel like Europeans; indeed, most of them seem to be thankful that they have nothing to do with that distressful continent. The political theories and ideas which are being tried out in Mexico are not European but American. The Revolution seems to have learnt nothing from Russia; while counter-revolutionary activities must be sadly disappointing to the Nazi and Fascist agents—such as the Italian prince who arrived in Cuba with the picturesque title of "Inspector of America". They have learned nothing from Europe, except violence; not even the use of castor-oil.

On this visit to Mexico I began to meet Mexicans of the older regime, those who look back to the reign of Porfirio Díaz as a golden age, because in subsequent revolutions they lost everything that they possessed. Hitherto I had only come across Mexicans belonging to the minority concerned with inviting some of my Spanish friends to Mexico; and they were generally leaders of Mexican thought and a long way ahead of most of their countrymen. They belonged to that group of "idealistic and genuinely patriotic Mexicans" described at the end of his book by Mr Stuart Chase; the type of men whose fathers had dictated the Constitution of 1917, who have forced reform after reform; have "fought—and died—for rural education, for public health, for the destruction of serfdom, for the economic independence of the village, for the restoration of dignity among their fellow citizens, for the cultural unity of Mexico". The group is small, but select. Its sense of leadership and its tangible achievements have been comparable with those of a kindred group in Spain—now scattered by General Franco with the approval of his smart but short-sighted friends in London. Mexico, in 1910, was "a feudal state with a few Victorian trimmings"; while the Mexicans I had been meeting were the younger members of the group which has "blocked out, and partially achieved, programmes in labour legislation, education, land reform, stimulation of the arts, national economic planning, as progressive as they are daring...". The Utopia of which these leaders caught a glimpse has (as Mr Chase felt obliged to point out) not been achieved. Indeed they have been forced time and again "to retreat from outposts already captured. Their ranks have been enfiladed by fire from the militarist, politician, *hacendado*, cleric, foreign capitalist. What they hoped to do in 1920 is decimated in 1931." The survivors from the Díaz regime, and their descendants, constitute a peculiar problem for Anglo-Mexican relations. They often possess a personal charm and a knowledge of English which is irresistible, so long as one is in their presence. Many of them were at school in England and sometimes at Oxford as well; they speak English perfectly and with complete naturalness and no diplomat can resist them. For the members of the British colony they are "the only decent people in Mexico", "the real Mexicans", "white men", "sahibs"; whereas, in reality, their Mexico (like their England) is a never-never land with a doubtful past and a still more doubtful future—the sort of country and the sort of social conditions which could only be restored and kept in being by a dictatorship.

It was all very well as long as Don Porfirio lasted. The age of Díaz, like the age of Queen Victoria and Edward VII, was a golden age for the large landowner and the foreign capitalist. But after the arrival—and assassination—of "poor Sr Madero", the landowning families (the *hacendados*) began to lose heavily, and what was not taken from them under the presidency of Carranza has been expropriated by the agrarian policy of President Cárdenas.

One is bound to have sympathy with these people. After all, we are coming to it ourselves, in England—in a different, if somewhat gentler fashion; and an English traveller in Mexico can only admire the fortitude with which many of the "new poor" Mexicans bear up under such misfortunes. One I met had lost not only a large estate in the north, but a small house and garden near Mexico City. Large estates in Mexico were often nice little properties in the neighbourhood of a million acres, an *hacienda* as large as a province;

while in England a man is considered to be a landowner on a ducal scale, if he owns a hundred thousand acres. The unkindest cut of all, however, was the loss of the garden near Mexico; for this had been the owner's own creation and handiwork, while the few other *hacendados* I met seemed to have no knowledge or interest in trees or plants, and one declared roundly that there were no flowers on an *hacienda*. There is at least one dispossessed *hacendado* who has firmly adopted an academic career, and by this time is a recognized authority on his own subject; while another is occupied in translating—of all things—the poems of Shelley. (But then, Shelley himself, much as he hated it, came of a family of *hacendados* in England.)

For the people I have mentioned—the exceptions—one can have nothing but sympathy and admiration. But for one philosophic mind which has accepted the situation, there are ninety-nine who sit about in bars and lend willing ears to the emissaries of Italy and Germany. Half the morning papers in Mexico City, and all the evening ones, seem to have been bought or influenced by totalitarian agents; and the dispossessed classes are a most valuable ally of the Nazi-Fascist reaction. Here, the men educated in England fall easy victims; for, with very few exceptions—I knew one exception who was at Rugby, and he was afterwards killed in Spain—the schools chosen for them were Stonyhurst and Beaumont, which in Mexico are supposed to represent the normal English public school tradition.

Mexicans have not perhaps a very clear idea of what the English public school tradition is, and have certainly not understood that one of its greatest and most characteristic products is the freak, who may one day become the "mad Englishman". In the case of Mexicans educated in England, their education has left them neither Mexican nor English; it has cut them off from both countries instead of making them a part of both; or rather (as far as England goes) it has made them part only of a fantastic and grotesque parody of England, where (as a Mexican himself told me, to illustrate the "variety and picturesqueness" of life at an English public school) you might run up against an Austrian archduke and a Bourbon prince discussing, in a heated but amicable fashion, which of the two should take precedence in an ecclesiastical procession. The atmosphere of an English public school is certainly peculiar; it would have needed nothing less than an Oscar Browning to cope with such a situation; but "O.B." (who, after all, was for many years a master at Eton) would probably have settled the question by making Austrian archdukes and Bourbon princes appear strictly in school order.

This, then, is the difficulty. These are the Mexican Anglophils; though they read and support newspapers with such Anglophobe headlines as could only have been inspired by Germany or Italy. They give British representatives a wrong, or at any rate one-sided, view of the Mexican people of to-day and modern Mexican idealism; while, to Mexicans, they give a totally inaccurate view of what the majority of British people to-day are saying and thinking. They are, again, definitely anti-American in feeling, and that makes it still more awkward for the British visitor who finds it possible to have good friends both in Mexico and the United States, and is not disposed to think that totalitarian solutions on the German or Italian model are the only ones worth consideration.

At the time I was in Mexico the British Empire had no official relations with Mexico at all, owing to a somewhat hasty gesture of the British Government over the question of oil. Such relations as there were were entirely the work of individuals; but individuals nowadays find it difficult to make headway against a daily stream of totalitarian misrepresentation, poured out by a press which (it is said) has been bought for thirty pieces of silver—or even less. Still, it is fortunate that, at the moment, totalitarian methods have no concern with culture, and (as that member of the Mexican Government expressed it, at a Christmas party), oil need not blacken our relations with our friends.

Mérida seemed to me a thoroughly Spanish town—one of the most Spanish towns I had yet seen in Mexico—and Spanish in the only way places in modern Mexico can be really Spanish: in its architecture and way of building. There is an arcaded plaza, with a rather nondescript renaissance cathedral on the north side and the colonial governor's palace, in the plateresque style, on the east. Behind the arcades on the south side are the Palacio Municipal and the University of Yucatán.

Above all, there was peace and tranquillity, especially noticeable after the din of Veracruz. There were a few tramlines, but no trams; the usual means of moving from one place to another, or for taking the air, seemed to be a race of curious, cubic, horse-drawn cabs, locally known as *púlpitos* or pulpits. Even the motor-buses seemed to go quietly and the few loud-speakers were strangely subdued. Men sat in patios, strumming guitars; and whether they sang, or put on a record or two to pass the time, it was rather hushed, with little or nothing of the peculiar, aggressive stridency of Havana or Veracruz. Commerce, however, has stepped in, to remedy the defect; and a combination slot-machine, loud-speaker and gramophone (apparently of Italian manufacture) has already been installed in the two principal cafés.

The proprietor and the boy Luis came to me at dinner, full of plans for immediate excursions. I put them off with talk of my letter of introduction; but the difficulty, obviously, was to be let alone to enjoy the peace of that delightful, easy-going, tropical town, without being rushed off at once to inspect Maya ruins. The next day was uneventful, and wasted (no doubt) in the eyes of the charming French count, who wanted me to go off the next morning on a five-day excursion to some little-known ruins in the south. "One sleeps in hammocks...!" Once more I produced my letter of introduction as an excuse. In that sense, it was the most useful letter of introduction I have ever had; though if it had been a botanist who had asked me to go with him, I felt that I should have gone like a shot. "But you can present your letter this afternoon; and, once that is done with, then...." I couldn't quite see myself doing such a thing, after twenty years' experience of Spain—presenting a letter of introduction on a Sunday afternoon at the private house of an important local official— and in the end I ambled up and down, taking numbers of photographs of old iron *rejas* and scenes in a market, watching the Maya Indians moving about in their white skirts with bands of bright embroidery round the top and bottom, listening to what they said and the clear, characteristic, and rather German way in which they pronounced the Spanish language.

The Yucatecans are well known in Mexico for their peaceable qualities. They are also rather good-looking, both men and women, in their calm, dignified, broadly smiling way. The hotel was run, it seemed, by well-favoured urchins like Luis; while the proprietor, who treated them all with an air of paternal affection, belonged to an old family of landowners, all educated in England he told me, except himself; though he, by an accident (he did not say, "a fortunate accident"), was educated in Paris. He deplored the break-up of the large estates of *henequén* (the English word is sisal, and it is a species of agave from which a rough twine is produced). The break-up of estates, he said, had paralysed the industry, greatly reduced the output, and, at the same time, the number of millionaires in the place.

There, I can offer no opinion. I am not an economist; and, in my home town, economics is taken far too seriously for an untrained person to make rash statements about it. What I was told about Mérida may be true; but that is always the kind of thing that is told to travellers, especially by hotel keepers. (It was in Spain, too.) On the one hand you have the local landlord and employer, or the inhabitant of an agricultural district, who cannot imagine that conditions anywhere else can be any different from the conditions he knows himself; while on the other is the central government, which it would be childish to regard as being without information

of this district and many others. "The President came here.
I told him. I said: '*Señor Presidente*, tax us as much as you
like; but if you give the land to the Indians, they will produce
nothing....' The land has been divided; the crop is a fraction
of what it was; there is hardly a millionaire left in the whole
Peninsula...."

I give it up. I suppose that at this point some travellers
would roundly curse the Mexican Government. I have not
the knowledge to do so. How do I know what the Government wants, what the Ministry of Agriculture wants, or what
the hard-working, hard-thinking President wants, in the best
interests of the Mexican people? Even a recent English
critic of modern Mexico (one who was first on a railway and
afterwards in oil) has to admit that President Cárdenas is
"passionately sincere and honest"; while he adds (with a
certain lack of grace perhaps, but it is obviously well meant)
that the President cannot be altogether a fool, because his
policy, so far, has been an outstanding success. So in these
agrarian problems, as in oil problems and railway problems,
I can offer no opinion. There is only one subject in which I
might, perhaps, be a judge of the President's policy: the
subject of Spain and Spanish refugees and the value of their
admission into Mexico; and on that, I should say that
President Cárdenas has been supremely right.

At last I presented my letter of introduction. The recipient
was a little grim at first; and it was only when I gave an imita-
tion of a German diplomat trying to sell his champagne
to an aristocratic client in England, that he relented and took
me out in his car. He also put me in the way of getting to the
Maya ruins at Chichén Itzá. It seemed that a car was going
on the next afternoon, with two Frenchmen and a German who
were flying down from Mexico City, and I hastily booked the
remaining seat, while my amused host gave me letters for the
manager of the guest house and the Director of the Excavations,
both of whom were to prove unusually kind and helpful.

Chapter XI

MAYA

The Mayas, the founders of Chichén Itzá, first appeared in the wet, tropical lowlands of Central America, and then, rather later, on the drier peninsula of Yucatán. Their culture (as Spinden points out) was made possible by their progress in agriculture; they discovered how to cultivate a moist, low-lying country where everything grows with exuberance, and at the same time to keep their fields clean of weeds and parasites. Up on the high plateau, the preparation of land for sowing had been comparatively easy; natural vegetation was scanty, and irrigation could easily be controlled. In the low-lying country, however, trees had to be felled and fast-growing bushes perpetually kept down, if a farmer was to get a sufficient return. The principal crops of the Mayas were probably much the same as those on the high plateau, the most important being maize.

Along the edges of the Maya area, in the State of Veracruz and in Honduras, specimens of archaic art have been found: little clay figures showing the transition in style between the archaic and the Maya. The earliest historical records for the Mayas go back to about 600 B.C. About the beginning of the Christian era they appear with a calendar in working order, and probably also with the knowledge of how to predict an eclipse. Their earliest cities were in Northern Guatemala and Western Honduras (Copán), while a little later they were established at Palenque, now buried in the tropical forests of the Mexican State of Chiapas. After about A.D. 300 these cities seem to have been abandoned, perhaps through some overwhelming epidemic like yellow fever. The forest closed over them, and the remains of the population migrated to the peninsula of Yucatán, where they enjoyed another brilliant period, some hundreds of years later, at Chichén Itzá (which had been merely a provincial town in the first Maya Empire) and Uxmal. Finally, after A.D. 1195, came a period of Toltec influence. The Toltecs may have been immigrants into Yucatán, with their capital at Uxmal; they may have been mere invaders, or they may have obtained Chichén Itzá as a reward for their intervention in a civil war. In any case, from that time on, the architecture of the city begins to show distinct Toltec influence; and above all, a stadium or ball court was built, with a "temple" at each end such as is often found in Toltec cities but which, among the Mayas, is only known at Chichén Itzá and Uxmal.

The first building one notices in Chichén to-day is an immense pyramid, erected by (or in honour of) the god or hero Kukulcan. *Kukulcan*, in the Maya language, means Plumed Serpent—the equivalent of Quetzalcoatl in Aztec. Quetzalcoatl, in fact, appears now to have been a Toltec leader who came to Yucatán towards the end of the twelfth century A.D. On the top of the pyramid, on one of the door jambs of the temple, is a bas-relief which may be a portrait of Quetzalcoatl-Kukulcan, with a long pointed beard; at the bottom of the main staircase, on the north side, are a couple of huge plumed serpents. The fair beard and the plumed serpent are both present together: two attributes inseparably connected with Quetzalcoatl.

The main stairway has ninety-one steep steps. There is also a stairway up each of the other faces of the pyramid; and as $4 \times 91 = 364$, it has been thought that the Big Pyramid may be a monument illustrating the Maya calendar. Further, since each face has nine terraces, divided by the stairway, these are supposed to designate the eighteen Maya months. On the terraces can be seen panels let into the masonry; there are fifty-two of these, and this number is said to represent the fifty-two years which must pass before the calendar is completed. These explanations may seem far-fetched, but they are typical of the symbolism employed by the older races of America.

On the terrace, at the top, was a temple which has now been reconstructed by the Mexican Government. The pyramid itself has been found to be only an outer cover, with a smaller pyramid inside it (as at Teotihuacán); a trapdoor leads to a marvellously preserved ancient temple which was covered up when the present structure was built. There are treasures in this temple; the greatest is a jaguar throne like those shown in the picture writing of Maya manuscripts, with a red body, eyes of green jade, and spots of green jade also.

A little farther on and to the right, is a mass of excavation and reconstruction carried out by the Carnegie Institute of Washington: it was once known as Mound No. 18, but now is the Temple of the Warriors. It was built on the top of an earlier and prehistoric temple; and its three colonnades have undergone complicated rebuilding at different periods. The square columns are sculptured on all the four sides; the sculptures were originally coloured, and on some of them traces of the colour still show. On most columns the carved design is in three parts. At the top is the sun god; a kind of scroll, with a human figure falling out of it. In the middle of the column is a warrior; while at the bottom is a curious mask of a human face in a serpent's mouth, framed by feathers, and standing on two bird's feet with wide-spreading claws. There are about sixty columns altogether, and no two figures of warriors are the same. In many cases the bas-reliefs are believed to be portraits of particular men; and they are shown in their particular masks: as a bat warrior, a serpent warrior or a jaguar warrior, as the case might be. The building was probably erected sometime after the Toltecs became the rulers of Chichén Itzá.

Not all the columns are sculptured with warriors. Some show sky bearers, atlantean figures or caryatides; figures with uplifted arms supporting the lintels or parts of the roof; others have representations of sorcerers shown as toothless old men with wrinkled faces. At the top of the steep staircase to the platform supporting the actual temple are two figures, each sitting on a serpent's head. These figures were banner bearers. The holes in their hands were for the flagstaffs; and when the building came to be restored, the remains of wood appeared in the holes.

A person with no head for staircases and pyramids (and no special training in archaeology) is hardly a good guide to the ruins of Chichén Itzá. So I can only mention what I found with the help of a large map which the kindly American director of the excavations had given me. Amongst other remains, to the south of the Temple of the Warriors is a columned structure called the *Mercado*, or Market. Here, the columns are mostly round, not square as in the Temple of the Warriors; and very few of them are sculptured. There is a "Chac Mool"—a half-sitting, half-reclining figure, with knees up, head to one side, and a bowl on his stomach; the figure is made of a peculiar stone which rings like a bell when you knock it. Beyond is a square court, with walls and a group of slender columns arranged round the sides of a sunken, paved area. Whatever its original use may have been, to-day it looks like a swimming pool.

Going back to the Pyramid and turning north and west of it, one finds remains in all stages, from heaps of stones lying on the ground, to carefully restored ruins like the Ball Court. There is a heap of what might be stone 75 mm. shells—the remains of the Temple of the Cones. There is a path through dry scrub, leading to the well in which scented virgins were sacrificed to the rain-god; and not far from this, and lying on the ground, is a huge square stone with a beautifully executed and well-preserved serpent mask, with the human face in the serpent's mouth, and the feathers above; though of a different type to those on the columns in the Temple of the Warriors.

A little to the west of where this stone is lying, is the Temple of the Eagles, and the Cemetery. Eagles and jaguars are carved on large panels just below the platform on which the temple once stood. Each seems to be eating a large pear which it holds realistically in its paw; but the pears are really human hearts, so that the temple dates from Toltec times, and belongs to a people whose form of human sacrifice was more grim and messy than merely throwing a bejewelled and half-drugged virgin to the bottom of a well. The cemetery has human skulls carved all round the walls. They are shown horribly skewered on poles, as real human skulls were in the Valley of Mexico. When the Toltecs took over Chichén Itzá they wished to do the same as they had been accustomed to do at home; but as there were not enough skulls to go round, not enough to decorate the cemetery, they had reluctantly to accept carved stone imitations instead.

Against the outside wall of the Ball Court is a small building which seems to have been restored and put together from stones carved in bas-relief. In front, between two square carved columns, is a seat or throne in the form of a jaguar. The right-hand column represents a priest, wearing a long skirt embroidered with a criss-cross pattern; the left-hand column shows a warrior. The bottom stone on each side is decorated with a mask. The inner walls, and especially the back wall, are covered with carving in low relief, showing files of Maya soldiers, with plumes on their heads and armed to the teeth with throwing-sticks, spears and darts, and protected by small shields and arm-pads.

The temple up the steps is the Temple of the Tigers restored a few years ago, from a tumbledown mound, by the Mexican Government. There are said to be plumed serpents, and a frieze of prowling jaguars, "so realistically carved that it does not take much imagination to see them actually walk". Well, well! The jaguar (*el tigre*) down below, with the human heart in his paw, was quite realistic enough to show how well the Mayas could carve jaguars.

Then comes the Ball Court. It is a vast place, about 500 ft. long and over 100 ft. wide. At the north and south ends are little buildings called—as most archaeological buildings seem to be called—"temples", but it would be more reasonable to think of them as grandstands. The long walls (that is, the east and west walls) each have a large projecting stone ring, set vertically into the middle of the wall, near the top. One of the objects of the game (the authorities say) was to knock a heavy rubber ball through the opening of this ring. The player who succeeded in performing this feat was allowed to claim any articles of clothing he liked from the spectators crowded along the walls.

As the two rings are exactly opposite one another, it might have been thought that a rope, or even a net, was stretched from one to another across the court; but such an explanation is not accepted by archaeologists, and there is, I believe, a miniature, or early sixteenth-century drawing, showing the game being played in the way already described.

When the long walls were restored, a wide, high bench was discovered along the bottom of each; and, where the spectators dangled their legs, there are panels of sculpture in low relief showing what the players looked like. Each set of carvings shows various teams of seven men, facing one another across a large central medallion decorated with a skull. There are something like eighty figures altogether. Their clothes, and even their expressions—their rather anxious expressions—are shown only too clearly; and when one comes to the last panel on the left, one realizes the reason for their anxiety.

The last panel on the left, the one at the south-east end, shows the captain of the winning side holding in his left hand the head of the losing captain, which he has just cut off. There is no getting away from it. In his right hand, he holds the long, curved knife he did it with, the knife made of obsidian—the volcanic glass which Aztecs and Toltecs used for making knives for human sacrifice. One can see, also, what clothes the players wore: a thin jacket tucked into a

Chichén Itzá: Temple of the Bas-reliefs

Chichén Itzá: Player in the Ball-game

broad belt; a short skirt or kilt reaching about half way down to their knees; below the belt, in front, a sash tied in a loop; and at the back, a small shield from which hangs a bunch of plumes. Their arms are covered by thick, cotton-padded sleeves; while one leg is usually different from the other, the left being more dressed for show, while the right is protected by a large, circular knee-pad and a high, padded shoe. Hanging round the player's neck, there is generally a breast ornament marked with a human head. Through their noses they usually have a nose-stick, which, in the carvings, looks like a moustache. The players' bats are tucked into their belts: the handles are generally sculptured with the head of a man, a jaguar or a parrot. The head of the defeated captain shows some gruesome religious symbolism. The seven plumes which seem to spring from it represent spurts of blood; but, on the wall itself, they can be seen to be serpents with outstretched tongues.

The remains at Chichén Itzá lie in three groups. Those so far described belong to North Chichén; the others are referred to as Middle Chichén and Old Chichén. Following the trail from North Chichén to Middle Chichén the first building one comes to is the Tomb of the High Priests. It is now a tumbledown temple, built on a squat pyramid; but there are remains of serpent balustrades, and—most important—an L-shaped block of hieroglyphics, giving a date equivalent to A.D. 1350. The tomb has been excavated, and apparently had been used for at least five different burials, the lowest in a natural cave. There were offerings of stone ornaments, and pieces of pottery. Farther along the trail is a curious, still roofed building, on a rather steep-sided platform which, however, it is easy to scramble up, for the view. The house is called the Red House, *Casa colorada*, because there were distinct traces of red paint on some of the stone panels. The Maya name, however, suggests that it was the town jail. From this building can be seen another small building on the remains of a pyramid: it is called the House of the Deer, but nothing much seems to be known about it. It shows the condition of remains in Chichén Itzá before they were excavated or restored.

Farther along the same track comes a group of buildings on which a good deal of work has been done: the Nunnery, or *Casa de las Monjas*. The name is connected with the legend which ended at the sacred well. The Nunnery was a girls' school, or women's college; and the legend is more or less as follows:

It was from among the most beautiful maidens studying there that many of the victims who were sacrificed in the well were selected.... The Mayans thought that the prolonged droughts which occasionally afflict the region were caused by the anger of Yum Chac, the Rain God, who was reputed to live at the bottom of the water.... They thought that much of his discontent was brought about through dissatisfaction with his present wife and that he needed a new one; so the priests selected from the Nunnery the most beautiful girl and she was married to the Rain God. For weeks preceding her sacrifice she was feted and prepared for her coming new life.... On the eve of the final day the girl was escorted with great pomp and ceremony to the Great Pyramid where she was anointed with a decoction of gum, jaguar fat, and certain plants that yielded a dark green colour.... After this rite had been performed, she was clothed in her bridal raiment of heavily embroidered cloth and decorated with much jewelry made of shell, jade, turquoise and gold. Just before she was escorted down the great north stairway of the Pyramid to the Sacred Way, she was given a powerful draft of a narcotic. On the great plaza, by the serpent heads, she was placed in a magnificent litter and carried along the road to a temple. Here she was placed in a small room built over a great incense burner which filled her chamber with the pungent fumes of burning copal.... To the cadence of a chant she was seized by four sacrificial priests, and swung far out over the brink of the well. The legend tells us that if she survived this plunge made at dawn and was swimming about on the surface of the pool at sunset, a rope was lowered to her and she was hauled up, to be treated for the rest of her life as a goddess living in human form. It is doubtful that many of the girls ever survived.

About forty years ago, someone decided to put the legend to the proof, and dredged the sacred well. "The many bones

Chichén Itzá: Temple of the Two Lintels

Uxmal (Yucatán): Gateway

brought to the surface bear mute witness to the number of girls who joined Yum Chac in his watery palace." There were also hundreds of gold and copper bells, thousands of jade beads, dozens of plaques made of jade, gold and copper.

In the group of buildings as seen to-day, the Nunnery is the one on the right. Immediately to the left is a building known as the East Annex. The panels on the lower part of the walls are of stone lattice-work. At the east end of the East Annex is one of the most beautiful pieces of decoration in the whole group of buildings. On each corner, and on each side of the door, are huge masks of the hook-nosed god, Itzamna; while over the door is a strange, plumed, sculptured figure.

Next to it is the building which has been called the *Iglesia*, the Church. There seems no reason why it should be called a church, except that in the minds of Spanish Catholics a Nunnery is generally associated with a church or chapel. The decorations on the walls of the building are characteristic. The lower band of the wall below the cornice was probably painted red. Above it is a band of decoration ending at the corners and meeting in the middle in the grotesque hook-nosed mask. These masks are strictly conventionalized. "The central hooked projection represents the nose, on each side of which is a highly stylized eye with ornamented eyebrows. The teeth shown in the gaping mouth are twisted and hooked, probably to indicate that they have been filed. Outside the eyes are huge square ear-plugs with a small circular projection from their centres and appendages probably representing feathers." It is unusual to find a mask like this over the doorway: generally they are placed at the corners. (F. Martin Brown, *A brief guide to the ruins of Chichén Itzá*, 1936.)

The remaining important building in Middle Chichén is the large structure with a round tower, known as the Caracol, or shell. It has been excavated by the Carnegie Institution in Washington, and is considered the most difficult and problematic of all the buildings in Chichén. During the excavations a hieroglyphic inscription was discovered; and though accurate decipherment has not been possible, the date is believed to correspond to A.D. 585.

The curious round tower has caused much discussion, for circular building among the Mayas was most unusual. It has been called an observatory. Measurements made at the upper windows seem to bear out this supposition, for it is possible to align the right inner jamb and the left outer one of the west windows and get a true line east and west. The south window can be used in the same way for a bearing which is true south. On March 21st, the vernal equinox, the sun sets exactly on the east and west line, and thus would mark the beginning of spring.

The third group of buildings, Old Chichén Itzá, is some distance away, a pleasant walk through dry, tropical scrub, passing the buildings of the Hacienda, which are the head-quarters of the Carnegie Institution. The first ruin one comes to has been called the Temple of the Dated Stone, all that is left of it being two Caryatides supporting a carved stone lintel. This lintel is the most important stone in the whole of Chichén Itzá, for it is the only one inscribed with a date in the unabbreviated system known as the Long Count, and the date has been read, without any possibility of error, as a formula corresponding to A.D. 619. This is the key date from which it has been possible to make an accurate correlation between Christian and Mayan chronology.

From the Temple of the Dated Stone, a path branches off to another little temple, which was undoubtedly concerned with naturalistic fertility rites; the Caryatides, which supported the lintel and probably represented priests, have loin-cloths with ornamental borders and long hanging tassels. A short distance farther on are the remains of the Temple of the Owls, with queer little owls carved on the few square columns which remain. Going back to the Temple of the Dated Stone, and farther along the same path, one comes to the Temple of the Caryatides. The two figures are actually at the back; and one comes straight up against an unrestored house with ancient Maya rooms just as they were found. In the first there is a stone bench at one end, and another along the south-west wall. They are long enough and wide enough to have been used for beds. The west wall is pierced by a doorway opening into a room about the same size but with no other opening. In the west wall of this dark inner room, and let into the stone-work above one of the beds is a colossal phallus "carved in the full round"; in other rooms there are other beds with other overpowering phallic symbols; and this "temple" (if it was not a mere bawdy house) must have been a temple of the oldest rite or the oldest profession.

A little farther on, as one passes by the Caryatides at the back gate of this "temple", is another building—also called a temple, though it is innocent of any obviously sinister purpose—the Temple of the Two Lintels. It is beautifully decorated and has been admirably restored by the Carnegie Institution. The scheme of decoration is in much the same style as that of the Nunnery; the stone lattice-work in the roof and at the base of the façade is like that forming the lower panel of the east wing of the Nunnery, while the zigzag design like fretwork above the doorways is another typical mode of Maya decoration. At the two north corners are striking examples of the hook-nosed mask, as fine as any to be seen in Chichén Itzá.

There is one other characteristic of Maya building which is perhaps more obvious at Uxmal than at Chichén—the Maya system of vaulting. The builders had not invented the keystone arch, but employed the vaulted arch instead. The knowledge of mechanics which such a structure involves is still con-siderable; and it is odd that such a people did not also discover the use of the wheel. Yet the technique of roofing a building in Mayan times seems, to say the least of it, to have been somewhat wasteful of time and labour. A building about 26 ft. long and only a single story high has the top of the roof over 30 ft. above the floor.

All this Maya art may seem strange and unintelligible at first; but when one looks at it long enough, wonderfully attractive qualities begin to appear in it, in architecture, decoration and sculpture. The Maya draughtsmen had considerable knowledge of foreshortening and composition. They could draw the human body in profile in natural and graceful attitudes, and they could enclose several figures in a rectangular panel, so that the result satisfies a modern eye for composition. But as we break away more and more from the shackles of our own artistic conventions (Spinden observes), we shall be better able to appreciate the many beauties of ancient American sculpture.

Maya art is dominated by the serpent motive, which became of the first importance in all subsequent art in Mexico and Central America. The serpent was seldom represented realistically; yet the original model was clearly a rattlesnake. Then parts of other creatures were added, such as the plumes of the quetzal bird, the teeth of the jaguar, and the ornaments of man. The serpent was idealized, and the lines characteristic of it entered into the delineation of many subjects distinct from the serpent itself. Scrolls and other sinuous traces were added to the serpent's body, and human ornaments, such as ear-plugs, nose-plugs, and even head-dresses were added to its head. Finally a human head was placed in its distended jaws. The Mayas must have intended to express the essentially human intelligence of the serpent in this fashion. "The serpent with a human head in its mouth doubtless belongs to the same category as the partly humanized gods of Egypt, Assyria and India. It illustrates the partial assumption of human form by a beast-divinity." (Spinden.)

The Mayas produced a real and coherent expression of beauty, and their influence was as important in America as that of the Greeks in Europe. Brought up, as we are, in the bonds of our own religious and artistic conventions, we may find it difficult to feel immediate sympathy for a form of beauty which is involved with an incomprehensible religion. Only when we can bring ourselves "to feel the serpent sym-

Chichén Itzá: Human face in jaws of Plumed Serpent

Chichén Itzá: Mask of Itzamná; The Hook-nosed God
(Temple of the Two Lintels)

bolism of the Maya artists as we feel, for instance, the conventional halo that crowns the ideal head of Christ", shall we be able to recognize the emotional qualities of Maya sculpture. The serpent, as in many parts of the ancient world, was a general indication of divinity, while the chief position in the Maya pantheon was held by the hook-nosed god, Itzamna. According to the early Spanish writers, Itzamna was the creator and preserver of all mankind, the inventor of writing, the founder of Maya civilization, the god of light and of life. His companion was Ixchel, goddess of the rainbow. There was a god of death, a maize-god, the Lord of the Harvest, a war-god of somewhat youthful appearance, as well as a more mature and more revolting war-god called the Black Captain. There was also a god whose face was a more or less humanized serpent.

The architecture and sculpture of this people have been described many times. A small book with admirable illustrations is Joyce's *Maya and Mexican Art*. (The Studio, 1927.) Their art has analogies with work in the Valley of Mexico. The Big Pyramid seems to have been built by Quetzalcoatl; it is, at any rate, the first building in which serpent columns and other structural ideas of that ruler were given artistic expression. The mausoleum of the high priests is a further development of the same style (A.D. 1339), while the large group of columns in the Temple of the Warriors may be even later. Finally, in the first half of the fifteenth century, civil war and disease led to the abandonment of the Maya cities of Yucatán, including Uxmal and Chichén Itzá.

Chapter XII

OPHELIA, DONNA ANNA, ELVIRA AND THE PEDREGAL

Chichén Itzá is four hours' drive from Mérida, over one of the most bumpy roads I ever remember. The other people in the car were French and German: two Frenchmen—brothers, *braves gens*, one an *industriel* and the other a doctor—and a young German who declared that he had spent three months travelling up the Pacific coast of South America, taking coloured photographs, and making, no doubt, certain observations required by his Government.

I had always imagined the place to be a tropical jungle; but the road, when it was not running through plantations of *henequén*, bumped along between miles of scrub and copse. There were no tall trees, but a dry and rather wilted tangle, with an occasional vividly green tree for contrast and a good number of flowering trees as well. It is not in Yucatán, but in Chiapas and Guatemala that the Maya remains are lost in impenetrable, tropical rain forest. The soil here is shallow; a little earth on the top of limestone, with underground streams and mysterious caverns. Once I saw a huge iguana lizard crossing the road.

The letter of introduction to the manager of the guest house helped me to get special consideration—a round thatched Maya hut in the garden, with the thatched roof sticking out for two or three yards all the way round, so that one could sit and scribble out of doors in the evening. Inside the hut everything was faultless, and beautifully kept; two beds with embroidered Maya counterpanes, and—in a sort of apse—

a white tiled gleaming bath-room with a shower which never ran dry. There were several other round huts like mine, each with an apse (which must also have been a bath-room); but the main part of "Mayaland Lodge" (as it was rather surprisingly called) was a two-storeyed building, consisting of bed-rooms with a balcony above, and a dining-room and "office", with a verandah, below.

The restaurant was served by very brown damsels in Maya garments, white with bands of embroidery, as at Mérida; but what diverted me, puzzled the other tourists and upset the archaeologists was a Mexican film company, making scenes for a Maya film with a background of the most famous (and most restored) monuments. The Mexican film stars looked amusing and the men looked companionable too. They would come into lunch, some of them, in their film clothes; one pair did so with all their war-paint on, made up as ancient Mayas of pre-Columbian times, when pure virgins were ceremoniously thrown into a well, and a captain of a side in the ball game would lose his head, if he lost the match. As a rule the men acting in the film appeared about the guest house in open shirts and flannel trousers; but there was evidently a superstition that riding breeches and solar topees were the right things for Yucatán. Two of the ladies affected this form of disguise. They were called Ophelia and Donna Anna. That, in itself, was sufficiently startling; but not even Bernard Shaw, I think, or Miss Sylvia Townsend Warner—the only other person in the world who could imagine a meeting between Ophelia and Donna Anna—would have had the idea of putting them both into riding breeches. Meanwhile their boy friends ran about in the heat after lunch, practising with a Maya throwing-stick. Arrows flew all over the garden, into the trees and under the thatch of the huts; until Donna Anna urged them to "have done, by yonder sun", and Ophelia was calling: "¡A descansar! You promised to come to bed!"

The author of the scenario was there at dinner. I had a letter to him, too—more in the capacity of postman than of

introduction, but it was pleasant to meet him, and the proprietor of the guest house suggested that, so far from being
"molested" by coming to talk to me, he found me a good
excuse for getting away from the leading lady of the film (who
was neither Ophelia nor Donna Anna). The author was a
Spanish poet and a teacher of the Maya language; for Maya
is a big subject, one of the four Indian languages in Mexico
spoken by over a quarter of a million people, and in some
parts of Yucatán it is said to be increasing at the expense of
Spanish. It also has a not inconsiderable literature, including
the collection of cosmogony and legends (written in the Maya
language but in Spanish spelling) known as the "Books of
Chilam Balam".

The great joy at Chichén Itzá (beyond the mere sightseeing)
was a visit to the Director of the Carnegie Excavations.
I gathered that the best time to call upon him was about
half-past eight in the morning. He heard my "Castilian"
Spanish from afar, and declared at once, with a great laugh,
that he would write to his cousin about it—his cousin being
Professor of Spanish in an important American University
and the greatest living authority on old Spanish ballads.

At that first interview the Director of Excavations did the
one thing most calculated to win my heart. He presented me
with an enormous map of the whole archaeological area of
Chichén Itzá. It was over 4 ft. long and 2 ft. wide, on a scale
of 1 : 3000, or 250 ft. to the inch. One could do something
with a map like that. With such a survey I was completely
independent of the authorized guide, the two Frenchmen
and the German colour-photographer. I could find my own
way about, dawdle, procrastinate, and take photographs
just as I liked; and once when I was challenged by a keeper,
it was enough to wave the map and shout: "¡Amigo del
doctor—!" Of course, if I had gone with the authorized guide,
the two Frenchmen and the German colour-photographer,
I should have noticed many more things. It takes a little time
to get used to the style of decoration; and it was only by

reading and looking at photographs between visits to the excavations that I realized how many things I missed on the first morning and how many things I had to go back and look for again.

At tea that afternoon the Director again won my heart by offering me weak tea—with many apologies. It was not only weak, but it was Lapsang Souchong; and I promptly declared that it was not true to say that all English people liked strong Indian tea.

The Director was working just then at a Maya family, the members of which can be traced from the year 900 down to the present day. At one time ruling princes of Uxmal, by the time of the Spanish conquest they were *caciques*; under the Spaniards, *hidalgos*; and since Mexican independence, gradually declining *milperos*—small farmers. He described how the family had kept the pedigree and all the papers; not for legitimate family pride, nor yet for mere snobbery, but because, whenever the head of the family died, or whenever a new Spanish Governor was appointed, it was essential for the family to prove their *hidalguía*—their being born and bred *hidalgos*—so that they might continue to enjoy the privileges which that state conferred: such useful privileges as exemption from taxation and the right to make Indians work for them. The fact of having to prove *hidalguía* so frequently led, naturally, to the production of a great many legal documents; and in the case of this particular Maya family, the documents not only exist, but can be checked with other family records and with the recollections of old members of the family, which the Director has been indefatigably collecting and collating for a considerable number of years.

I spent the mornings in going to the ruins, in every direction. It was delightful to start early—before 8.30—and walk alone, with no guide except the map, through the dry, scrubby woods. Birds were singing; but there was no other sound beyond the quick, dry crackle of a lizard or a snake, disappearing into the undergrowth. I caught sight of several lizards, but no snakes, though I thought I could distinguish the sounds made by each. These mornings were delightful, fresh and not too hot. There was one slight mishap, but it fortunately led to nothing. It was in the Temple of the Two Lintels. There are three rooms, and I had been conscientiously into the first two and was inspecting the third. Lying on the floor was one of the curious knee-shaped stones, used by the Mayas in their system of roofing. But I confess that I was more curious to see whether there were any more phallic symbols. After those carved Caryatides of priests deliberately and archly showing what priestly garments usually hide (but what, I suppose, every worshipper went to that particular temple to see), and after that other "temple", with its low stone divans as broad as beds and the startling phallic stones projecting from the walls, I thought that there might be further surprising objects in this remote Temple of the Two Lintels. Instead of that, there was a high, characteristically "wasteful" Maya roof, with wasp's nests hanging from it. I was looking at one nest, carefully not standing directly underneath it, when from another nest, Nemesis fell into my eye in the shape of a wasp. I thought at first it was a sting and wondered what the Maya remedy would be. (*Mud*, Mrs Director said afterwards.) But as time went on and nothing further happened, it was clearly only a bruise, caused by a wasp of a certain weight falling from a high Maya roof with an acceleration of 32 ft. per second.

In the afternoon I went to tea with the Director again. He was working at his Maya family tree, a thing even larger than my map, showing the descent and fortunes of the family for rather more than a thousand years. I noticed that about three-quarters of the present generation had died young, and the Director agreed. Infant mortality among the Mayas of to-day is about 75 per cent.

Next day I left Chichén about 3 with the manager of the guest house and all his family in a smallish car. However, we arrived safely at Mérida just as it was getting dark. There was no seat in the aeroplane for five days; still there was the Maya City of Uxmal to be seen, and an afternoon excursion to the Port of Progreso. Wise people coming this way will prefer "Progress" to the "True Cross", and get off the boat at Progreso instead of going on to Veracruz and flying back. But I had had my refugee to consider, and there was no other choice. Progreso had nothing much beyond a delicious sea breeze, and surf bathing, for those who had villas in which to leave their clothes, or friends on the beach to look after them. I saw nothing in the way of a bathing hut. Opposite the station and under the hotel "Diligencias" was a bookshop full of the things one used to see twenty years ago in Spain, but which had been gradually disappearing from the bookshops.

Although I did not know it, a high authority in Mexico City had written to two local archaeologists to look after me; though he had omitted to tell me to go and call upon them. It was only by accident that someone found out, and took me to see them. The result was a visit to Uxmal in the Government van, leaving at 5.30 a.m. and returning about 12 hours later. As it only takes about a couple of hours to get there, in any case, and over a far better road than the one to Chichén, it would have been more satisfactory and less exhausting to have taken a taxi. When the morning came it was dull and soon turned to rain; an ideal day for the Government archaeologists and the diggers, but disastrous for me, as it made photography difficult or impossible. I am not an expert photographer; but I realize that what makes a good photograph is not the light but the shadows; and here I was, at a place where the Maya schemes of decoration would have provided marvellous effects of shadow, if only there had been a little direct sunlight. The two Government archaeologists were as kind and friendly as possible, but it was on the whole a tiring and unsatisfactory day. Next morning, when I left in the plane for Mexico City, it was gloriously fine and clear. I went straight through, leaving Fortín and Córdoba for another time.

When I passed that way again, it was the rainy season, and by that time even the plains and steppes of the high plateau were full of flowers; indeed the rainy season is, to my mind, the most beautiful of all the Mexican seasons. Prickly pears and the lines of unattractive agave plants, which in winter had been growing wretchedly on a brown, burnt-up soil, were now sticking up out of a mass of vivid greens, with here and there patches of yellow or orange daisies, crimson *Bouvardias*, *Oxalis*, *Ipomoea*, *Tacoma* and dozens of others. The pepper tree, *arbol del Perú*, was everywhere, but seemed rejuvenated; the maize was standing high and very green.

You leave Mexico City early and spend the whole morning rumbling along through this sort of landscape, until suddenly, at Boca del Monte, the train gets to the edge, and in a few minutes you find yourself in a different world. The train begins to coil down the mountain side through oaks and pines, ferns, orchids and evergreens, and patches of green grass. Orizaba is still 4000 ft. above sea-level. Córdoba 2700 ft.; while Fortín, between the two, is about 3320 ft. It is a semi-tropical Eden, with an excellent hotel, a fabulous view of the Pico de Orizaba, and an Indian population which (like a small, brown acquaintance of mine, Elvira González) spends most of its time selling gardenias and orchids whenever a train stops at the station. "¡ *Ya viene!*" A bell clangs mournfully from a monstrous electric engine, and a long corridor train draws up at the platform, while Elvira and all her brown-faced, white-frocked friends surge towards it with both arms raised and an enormous bunch of gardenias in each hand. There are not many trains, and not every passenger, I am afraid, has the sense to respond to Elvira, her soft voice, or her gardenias. But her flowers are packed up in moss and ferns and a thick section of bamboo stem, and will keep fresh till the end of the journey, the next train, or even till to-morrow; for the thick piece of bamboo will shut as tightly as a tin, and is nearly the same shape as the old-fashioned tin botany box.

In the comparatively short railway journey from Mexico

City to Fortín, or Veracruz, one meets with every kind of
country, from the dry, cool plateau up above to the tropical
swamps on the coast. The best description of the journey I
have seen is the one given by the late Dr Gadow of Cambridge; his book *In Southern Mexico* is one of the best, though
one of the most neglected works, every written on Mexico by
an Englishman. Gadow, though he was primarily interested
in frogs, toads, newts, lizards and snakes, revelled in the coffee
and banana plants round Orizaba; the *Anona* trees, with their
charming fruit and charming name, *Chirimoya*; the occasional
palms, the yuccas fencing the homesteads, the flaming red
Hibiscus blossoms sticking out their pistils at you, and the
large, white trumpet-shaped flowers of *Datura*, smelling
sweetly at night. He noted the striking mauve or pink flowers
of the banana; the pineapple growing wild; the alligator pear
or *aguacate* with its long oval fruit so much used in Mexican
salads; and the *zapote* which (he declared) was a name used
for almost any kind of fruit that is succulent and has a few
large seeds.

Every day that I was in Fortín, and indeed on most days of
the year, there was a belt of cloud on the north-east and south
side of the mountain, whilst the west was dry; but those north
winds (one of which I had experienced at Veracruz during the
dry season) come raging in from the Gulf, and veil Jalapa,
with most of the uplands of the State of Veracruz, in a drizzling
rain, which lasts for days together. The hot air (as Gadow
explained) travels inland, saturated with moisture from the
sea, and then rises, causing the cool air from the mountain
fringe of the plateau to rush underneath, and thus form the
clouds which send down the torrential rains upon the low-
lying coast lands. As a rule, the whole of the morning at
Fortín was fine. But the moisture from yesterday's rain rises
from the warm soil in the form of vapour, and travels inland
until it reaches the cooler regions of the mountains, when these
districts get their daily thunderstorms. This may happen at
any hour between noon and late in the evening, according to

where one is, and so regular is it that in many localities which Gadow visited, invitations to afternoon or evening parties were issued with the reminder "after the storm".

It is inaccurate to say that during the rainy season it rains every day, either in Mexico City or on the slopes such as at Fortín, but during the wet season it certainly rains every other day on an average, and from one to three hours. At Córdoba, Fortín or Orizaba the annual rainfall is measured not in inches but in feet. Córdoba has about 8 or 9 ft. of rain in the year, and the soil is of incredible fertility, with every kind of tropical fruit and flower growing there in profusion.

Up in Mexico City the rainfall cannot be measured in feet, yet it makes a considerable difference. The pale, translucent morning sky of the wet season is gradually filled with piles of sailing cumulus clouds; the sun goes in about lunch time (Mexican lunch time) and the rain may come down at any time between four and eight. It does not necessarily rain every day, but one may expect it three days out of five. At the end of June, when the dry weather breaks, one may expect it to rain oftener; yet the mornings in Mexico are almost always fine; and one can see every morning how yesterday's downpour has freshened things up and brought new things out.

It was about this time, the beginning of a rather early rainy season, that I discovered the Pedregal (the "stony place"), an old lava bed near Mexico City, between San Angel and Coyoacán, which can be reached in about an hour by the tram. It is an entirely volcanic district, many square miles in extent, consisting of the solidified lava streams of a prehistoric eruption, which happened just lately enough for the remains of some of the earliest inhabitants of the Valley of Mexico to have been caught and buried beneath it. The direction and spread of the main lava streams can still be recognized by experts; while on cooling and weathering they have split into innumerable clefts and caverns which make ideal places for animals and plants.

It is not the case here, as it has been with other eruptions, of trying to discover which plants are the first to colonize a whole countryside blotted out by lava. That was done by Gadow at Jorullo, where the eruption only took place at the end of the eighteenth century; and Gadow was able to follow out the order in which plants gradually returned as colonists to the devastated area, comparing contemporary records of the eruption, the observations of Alexander von Humboldt in 1803 and all other accounts, down to the time of his own visit in 1908. His book was only published posthumously in 1930, but though regarded as a classic of its kind in Europe, it seemed to be completely unknown in Mexico.[1]

On the Pedregal it is no longer a case of trying to make out which plants are comparatively recent arrivals. Brown and bare as it looks in the dry season, as soon as rain begins to fall the whole place becomes a rock garden; and a rock garden with an infinite variety of situations in which plants can grow, from exposed positions on the surface, which are always dry even in the wettest months, to perpetually damp and cool retreats in hollows and clefts. This probably explains the bewildering number of plants to be found on the Pedregal; moisture remains permanently in the hollows, and so, even in the driest part of the year, roots can still find something to absorb. Animal life also profits by these varied conditions; there are numbers of insects: butterflies and small dragonflies; but, by a beneficent dispensation of Providence, there seems to be an absence of biting flies—even so late as the middle of August, when I went to the Pedregal for the last time. September, however, may be another story. There are said to be foxes in the holes and bats in the caves, and even rattlesnakes gliding between the hot stones; but though I kept a careful (if untrained) eye open for the possible presence of snakes, I never saw one.

The Pedregal is most easily approached from San Angel, near the Obregón Monument, described in an earlier chapter;

[1] Hans Gadow, *Jorullo* (Cambridge University Press, 1930).

and San Angel is itself one of the most flowery suburbs of Mexico. Most people who live there have gardens, and must find something in the soil or situation which makes it more amenable to plants than other environs of Mexico City. In July and August the smallest garden overflows with the flowers which were grown as choice rarities by English gardeners on the Riviera; but here they grow together in a riotous confusion which would have made the owner of a villa at Nice or Alassio almost uncomfortable. At San Angel, again, cultivated plants escape from gardens and can be found growing at the sides of roads or on pieces of waste land; while sometimes the opposite has taken place, for at least one conspicuous piece of waste land is known to have once formed part of a large garden. Some escaped garden plants have become weeds—an example is a low, bushy *Buddleia*; while at one period all the streets and plazas were full of something which looked like a buttercup, but was really a composite— called by Dr Reiche, *Lindheimera mexicana*. (His *Flora excursoria del Valle de Mexico* was one of the books I found secondhand in Mexico City.)

The edges of the Pedregal near San Angel are being eaten away by quarries and befouled by quarry villages. This is a pity; but it will take many years of such nibbling to make any great impression on the Pedregal itself; while from San Angel you get straight on to the Pedregal at its driest and most characteristic part. The only tree, to all intents and purposes, is the pepper tree, the *arbol del Perú*. It is of no great size, but appears in curious and unexpectedly beautiful shapes, with a background of uneven, bushy lava field, a line of jagged mountains and a dramatic sky, piled high with heavy white clouds. The most usual bush is a gigantic ragwort (*Senecio praecox*) which has developed a woody trunk and branches. I never saw it in flower, for its large yellow or pink blossoms come before the leaves in February or March. The leaves begin to appear in June, and their intense green is, I think, mainly responsible for converting the Pedregal from a predominantly brown place to a predominantly green one. It is a plant which stores water in its own stem; and it has a very individual look, through its stiff branches and bunches of leaves, standing out against the mounting masses of cumulus cloud.

Occasional rains at the end of May brought out a Zephyr lily (*Zephyranthes*) with pinkish white blossoms which seemed to become deeper in colour the longer they were out. June added various wood-sorrels (*Oxalis*); yellow, like the "weed" which has escaped from gardens at Tangier, only larger and finer, or else various shades of violet. There is also a red wood-sorrel, with gorgeous clusters of crimson flowers, often grown in Mexican gardens; but I do not remember seeing it on the Pedregal. The most attractive crimson flower, which grows abundantly on the Pedregal, in waste land round Chapultepec and in many other places—indeed it must be one of the commonest summer flowers in Mexico—is *Bouvardia*, with whorls of crimson, trumpet-shaped flowers an inch long. In July there are also various different kinds of convolvulus, some of which hide away out of the direct light of the sun, whilst others shut up during the morning, or only come out in the late afternoon, like the deep pink "Four-o'clock", *Mirabilis jalapa*, which also is a favourite plant in Mexican gardens.

The great month for the Pedregal, however, was August. The July flowers were still out, but had been joined by numberless blossoms which neither I nor an experienced, flower-loving friend, could identify. There were several members of the potato family; a lilac-blue salvia; *Ipomoea*, the purple "Morning Glory"; *Tagetes erecta*, the "Aztec marigold", and a smaller one, as well as the "French marigold" which many people grow in England. There were other flowers here which one remembered from English gardens: gaillardias, zinnias, a begonia, pentstemon, *Cuphea*, and above all, single dahlias; for Mexico, as it happens, has been the original home, and has now provided gardens all over the world, with some of the most striking and familiar flowers. The dahlia was named in honour of Andreas Dahl, a Swedish botanist and pupil of Linnaeus, by one of the foremost Spanish botanists of the eighteenth century, and director of the Botanical Gardens at Madrid, Antonio Cavanilles. Liberal, enlightened Spain has never had justice done to it; and the early Spanish botanists certainly contributed to that enlightenment. The dahlia was already known, before this time, to Dr Hernández, physician to Philip II, who wrote the first account of the plants and animals of the New Spain; and to Vicenté Cervantes, director of an eighteenth-century botanical garden in Mexico City, which has now vanished. Cervantes, towards the end of the eighteenth century, sent to the Botanical Garden at Madrid seeds of one of the bush dahlias growing wild in Mexico. From Madrid some seeds reached England; but the plants died and had to be reintroduced later. Seeds were also imported by a French botanist, but the flower did not interest gardeners much, until, in the seventies of the last century, it was introduced once more by way of Holland. It is probably from this date onwards that dahlias have been so dressed up by growers as to become almost unrecognizable—to make, at any rate, their wild country cousins in Mexico almost unrecognizable, if it were not for the single dahlia which, by itself, is such a superb flower that it has still held its own in Europe. The sight of single dahlias growing wild in Mexico was, to me at any rate, no less exciting than masses of new varieties at Kew or Hyde Park. Some species are definitely trees; others are high bushes, and the flowers are almost always out of reach, even of a camera. Yet it is from one of these that the single and double garden dahlias are said to be descended. Afterwards, at Pátzcuaro, I saw one or two flowers which showed signs of becoming doubled; but I never saw, anywhere, growing wild, a cactus dahlia; and this seems generally to be treated as a different species and named after President Juárez (*Dahlia jaurezii*), or is descended, or hybridized, from a wild cactus dahlia found in Guatemala.

The history of the discovery and cultivation of dahlias has been more or less repeated in the case of *Bidens, Cosmos,* and marigolds. Both the "French" and "African" marigolds are really natives of Mexico, where they still grow wild, in varying shades of yellow, sometimes flecked with orange or light brown. Zinnias, too, were growing wild everywhere on the Pedregal in August, bringing together unlikely and impossible combinations of colours, and yet showing that they would go very well together in Mexican sunshine. One wild zinnia has cardinal red petals and a yellow centre; a larger, orange one, gets mixed up with the blue, purple or magenta flowers of Morning Glories.

A striking wild thing of Mexico is the *Tigridia,* a lily of great distinction which only lasts for a day or so, but increases so rapidly that people who have taken it into their gardens sometimes wish they had not. Many *Ipomoeas* also are native to Mexico. There are any number of them in any number of shades and they bring to some minds once more the gardens of Nice and the Riviera. In Mexico, however, it is the wild flowers which provide the most startling contrasts. You do not see those pastel shades which we get in England. But pastel shades want an English sky to carry them off; and my first sight of the stalls in the Cambridge market, after coming from Mexico, was not a disappointment. A country's flowers get the sky they deserve.

Chapter XIII

LECTURE TOUR WITHOUT LECTURES

I got back to Mexico City at the end of April, to find more Spanish friends than there had been in December. Yet the general exodus of Spaniards from Europe had not yet begun, and many people I knew, and former members of my college in Madrid, were still shut up in concentration camps in the south of France. The only thing to do was to see as much as possible of those who were already in Mexico, and make oneself useful if one could. There was not always much chance of even doing that. An opportunity of a kind soon presented itself, however; though for me it was pure enjoyment and a most interesting experience. I found that two of them were going on a lecture tour to a place which at first I could hardly find on the map; and it seemed quite natural, both to the Spanish lecturer and to the Mexican organizer, that I should go too. Needless to say I jumped at the notion; it would be a combination of travel and sight-seeing with making new friends and "establishing cultural relations".

Guanajuato, the place which had asked for the lectures, proved to be a large, but extremely picturesque mining town, with a University College which hopes one day to become the State University. It is a ten hours' journey north of Mexico City, has a population of about 20,000 (66,000, however, in the municipal boundary), and lies 7000 ft. above the sea. It is surrounded by mountains, and its narrow, winding streets seldom remain at the same level for long. Yet they are noticeably clean and well kept; and the houses, and particularly the picturesque corners—often with niches (*hornacinas*) for saints, with little lanterns hanging in front of them—are well cared for and greatly admired. Guanajuato is, in fact, the most decorative town I saw the whole time I was in Mexico.

We arrived after dark, but had a great reception at the station; the Rector of the College was there, and various others including the Professor of Music and the Professor of English. There were five of us altogether, including the Spanish lecturer and his wife, and a Mexican singer who was to provide the musical illustrations. She was an excellent musician, one of the few singers I have ever heard who never, by any possible chance, sang out of tune; and her technical ability may be appreciated from the fact that she afterwards sang, at one of Chávez' symphony concerts, the soprano solo in the selection from Alban Berg's *Lulu*. But "Irmita" (for we eventually got as far as Christian names in the diminutive) was not going to trust herself alone, in a part of Mexico she didn't know, with three wild and unscrupulous Europeans. So she brought her maid with her; and we were all five conveyed to a small but attractive hotel with balconies looking on to a square with clipped, shrubby trees.

The next morning the square proved to be a small, three-cornered public garden with a bandstand in the middle of it. On the shortest side was the theatre, a neo-classic building in two shades of pink, with a row of bronze statues along the top. Next to it was a baroque church with a pink Churrigueresque façade, a pink tower and a pink dome. The pavement round the plaza garden was of alternate squares of bottle green and dark blue; the balconies of the hotel had shining silver balls at the corners, while looking up a steep and crooked street to the left (past a sign which said "Take Montezuma beer") one saw a high place on a hill of reddish earth. Inside, the hotel was built round a small, covered court. There was a marble-floored gallery, with a large blue Persian cat prowling round it; and the chamber-maid—an Aztec idol with gold teeth—declared that it had several *chicos*. The main object of the gallery, however, seemed to be to hang cages of canaries and other birds, yellow and blue, which never ceased twittering (except at night, when they were covered up), and served the purpose of providing a perpetual cheerful noise, which, in a more sophisticated establishment, would have been replaced by the less cheerful, crooning noises of a perpetual loud-speaker.

The State College of Guanajuato, at which my friend was to lecture, was originally a Jesuit foundation, now (like my own pre-Reformation college in Cambridge) converted to what I am bound to consider better uses. It began in 1732 as a *Hospicio y Escuela*, a hospice and a school, in a house given by a rich widow. In 1744, Philip V raised it to a *colegio*, with more gifts from the foundress and generous benefactions from a wealthy Basque. After the expulsion of the Jesuits from Spain and the whole of the Spanish Empire, under Carlos III —one of the greatest kings Spain ever had—the foundation at Guanajuato became the Royal College of the Immaculate Conception, giving instruction in all preparatory subjects, and special courses in Mining and Jurisprudence. Under an enlightened master, Don Juan Antonio de Riaño y Bárcena, a chair of French was established, aided by *tertulias* (conversation circles) which the master established in his own house. He also introduced (or established on a firm basis) teaching in Mathematics—originally the college seems to have been little more than a theological seminary—and invited as director of mathematical studies a Spanish or Mexican professor, José Antonio Rojas, who had the distinction of having been tried by the Inquisition.

The existence of these two chairs, of French and Mathematics, shows that the college was fully in line with the educational tendencies of the time; and about 1798, "the youth of Guanajuato, familiar with the French language and with the vivid personality of the Professor of Mathematics, was in a position to appreciate—more than any other in the country, and not excluding the capital itself—the contemporary ideal of liberty and the rights of man; thereby preparing itself for the Mexican struggle for emancipation which began in 1821 ".

Guanajuato was actually one of the first places to rise against Spain with Padre Hidalgo; but from 1821 to 1827 the college had to be closed. It was temporarily converted into a mint, though some of its lecture-rooms were kept open thanks to the labours and sacrifices of an unusually patriotic priest who had originally been a member of the college. In 1828 the college was solemnly reopened. Departments of Law and Mining Engineering were organized under a head who now had the title of Rector. Medicine began in 1835 (though this department was closed in 1892); and the college now consists of Preparatory, Secondary and Technical Schools, with departments of Law, Social Science, Engineering, Chemistry, Metallurgy, Economics, Commerce, together with first-aid instruction in hospital work and obstetrics. There is a pleasant, well-arranged and well-catalogued library of 30,000 volumes, and an important meteorological observatory, fitted (I was interested to see) with instruments by Negretti and Zambra, London.

Once we were in Guanajuato there was not much time for preparing lectures, or even for putting the finishing touches, or rehearsing the singer. The subject was concerned with the folk-lore of Spain; and, in spite of distractions and excursions, the fact that the room was difficult to speak in and that the lantern did not arrive until the last day, I have never heard a presentation of the subject that pleased me more. The lecturer had quite got away from the "pretty-pretty" sentimentality so usual in Spain when talking of folk-lore and "folk-ways". He is a folk-lorist who is not only concerned with the past but is aware of a "folk-lore present" and a "folk-lore future". He brought to his study of the subject (though without obtruding it upon our patience) a knowledge of musical history, psychology and comparative religion; he must be one of the very few Spanish folk-lorists who has ever heard of *The Golden Bough*.

At any rate, here at Guanajuato (as afterwards in Mexico City, when my friend lectured on the subject again) a beginning was made; and the way shown in which Spanish literary subjects should be approached, for it is a most important side of all Spanish writers: folk-lore, primitive customs and comparative religion. Mexican scholars, of course, know this very well. Some of the earlier Spanish friars—a few of them at any rate—were more concerned to preserve than to destroy. Padre Sahagún and his assistants, P. Mendieta and others, made marvellous collections of pagan traditions, though unfortunately their superiors (Archbishops Zumárraga and Landa) zealously destroyed and burnt every Aztec and Maya manuscript they could find. Sahagún and his assistants were struck by the obvious similarity between certain members of the Aztec and Catholic pantheons; and as a practical application of this, when a Catholic church was built on the ruins of an Aztec temple or Toltec pyramid, a Catholic saint was found to take over the functions and duties of the Mexican god who had formerly been worshipped there. Idols behind altars. Under this title Miss Anita Bremer has published some of the evidence on this subject; Hans Gadow did the same, thirty years ago; and Mr Rodney Gallop has just brought his great experience of folk-lore to the subject in a book (*Mexican Mosaic*) on which I must not trespass—almost the only modern English book on Mexico which may be considered fair and reasonable. A reasonable and musical approach to Spanish folk-lore was therefore the only one likely to go down with a Mexican audience (or those members of a Mexican audience who mattered); and I was delighted to find that my friend had adopted such an attitude in these lectures at Guanajuato.

My own job on this occasion was not to give lectures but to make friends. That was not difficult. It caused considerable surprise in Guanajuato that any English-speaking person could speak Spanish at all, let alone an Englishman from Europe. The English in Mexico have not a good reputation as linguists; and certainly such Spanish as I heard from them was devoid of any sort of construction, rhythm or intonation, and had an accent you could cut with a knife. My own experience of three visits to Spanish America has led me to suspect that difficulties between English concerns and Spanish-American governments are almost always due to inadequate knowledge of the language. Even our Mexican difficulties might be smoothed away, if the English people concerned knew enough Spanish, and took the trouble to speak it with the fluency, courtesy and grace which one Spanish American expects of another. Our cultural relations with Spanish America depend too much on Spanish Americans who speak English, and not enough on English people who speak Spanish. Our Universities can provide the necessary training —even in purely Spanish-American subjects; but the position of Spanish in British Universities depends ultimately on the policy of the schools. If these drop Spanish out of the curriculum, Spanish studies in Great Britain will be crippled, and crippled at the very moment of their greatest national importance. Dropping Spanish may seem an economy for the time being, but it is the most short-sighted policy imaginable; for, though no one can foresee the consequences of the present war, one thing at least seems certain—the immense increase in the power and prestige of the American continent, including that considerable part of it which speaks Spanish. I have no illusions about my own capabilities. I have listened to myself speaking Spanish into a dictaphone, and know that there are certain sounds which I cannot make correctly. But I am fluent, and like talking; and one's own pleasure in doing a thing that one can do easily probably makes one's hearers take the will for the deed. On this occasion, when the Professor of English was present, I made a great point of speaking to him in English—the best and clearest English I could command, especially in the presence of any of his colleagues; but otherwise, I had to talk to everyone else in their own language, and our "cultural relations" were certainly improved by doing so.

Guanajuato, as a great mining centre, is naturally a place for engineers. On our excursions, it was the engineer who made the arrangements and conveyed us in his car. He was always *el señor ingeniero*, or *el ingeniero* "So-and-So". Mexico likes to give every man his due, in titles as in other things; so you hear *el licenciado* for a man with a degree in law and a licence to practise: *el doctor* for a doctor of medicine or anything else. Even the Rector of the College was sometimes *el doctor*, though more frequently he was *el señor Rector*; and when the time came for us to be received by the Governor of the State, he was *el Señor Gobernador*.

The engineer was a man of curious and quick-witted charm. He thought of everything, and more particularly of ways in which we might enjoy ourselves; but, as was not unnatural, all his thoughts revolved around problems of engineering. Guanajuato owed its foundation to the engineers who had developed the mine, and it owed its existence—its preservation from floods—to the engineers who had planned the drainage. So the first excursion our engineer planned for us was to visit the reservoirs—*las presas*. It sounds a very engineering thing to do; but its primary object was to show us marvellous views of the place and the country round. The first stop—and I wish we could have stopped oftener, for photographs—was the Church of the Valenciana. It belongs to the second half of the eighteenth century, and is in the Churrigueresque style, with incredibly rich, golden retablos covered with carving and glowing dully with the soft-lighted surface which Churrigueresque gilt wood carving always produces. The church is named after the silver mine, one of the most celebrated in Mexico; and the munificence of the lucky mine-owners ran to a complete monastery (Colegio de los Teatinos) as well as to an enormous church. Beyond the church, and over a high ridge of hills (Cerro de Tomates), is a large reservoir, the Presa de la Esperanza, shut in on one side by a huge stone wall (100 ft. high in some places), with a road on the top of it. On the other side of the road, in a deep hollow, was a casino: a kind of country club, with a wild, shady garden. Lower down, there is another reservoir, really part of the town and joined to it by more gardens; and there are other reservoirs as well, built one above the other. The reservoirs used sometimes to overflow and the town was flooded; while the river running through the streets also overflowed its banks. Now the river is covered in, and has become itself a succession of streets; and a tunnel has been cut to divert the overflow from the reservoirs, a triumph of engineering.

On another day the engineer began by taking us up to the cemetery, on a hill to the south-west of the town. It has a glorious view; but the chief objects of the visit—objects that we were none of us particularly anxious to see—were the mummies of the recently dead, for which Guanajuato (through the extreme dryness of the air) is rather gruesomely famous. I was told privately that the engineer had himself mummified the body of his own father, and was not at all averse from showing his own handiwork—another triumph of engineering. The most striking thing in the cemetery, after the view from the gate—with the town lying below in a circle of grim, hard-outlined mountains—was a *Bougainvillea*, growing by itself, as a tree; not climbing, but overshadowing the grave of an American woman, with enormous green and black swallow-tail butterflies fluttering over the flowers.

Then, still in cars, we went up and down some of the mountains to the south of the town, ending in a rather perilous ascent of 1000 ft. above. I longed to get out and walk, as there was a delightful breeze, and it was not too hot for walking. But in a car we certainly covered more ground in a shorter time, and got more points of view than we should have done otherwise. Returning to the town by another road, we were taken to see an excellently installed orphanage.

Guanajuato is definitely the "other" Mexico. It is picturesque to the last degree—more so, even, than Taxco; yet at the same time it is clean and well kept, and the inhabitants take an interest both in schools and gardens. Though a haphazard, medieval looking town in its plan—so different, in that respect, from the regularly planned Mexican towns with all the streets at right angles—it has made room for squares with gardens in them, planted trees and flowers, realizing, as M. Georges Duhamel has done, that "la plus grande beauté d'une ville n'est pas dans les édifices, elle est dans l'espace libre entre les édifices". And with gardens and schools, there go libraries. In the square opposite the hotel there is a library for children only.

On the day before we left, we were received by the Governor. The Rector of the College came to fetch us about 11.30 and conveyed us to the Governor's official residence. He looked somewhat battered, but was distinctly friendly; while his private secretary might have come straight out of the Foreign Office in Whitehall. Then we were taken to pay our respects to the Governor's family next door, in a severely beautiful neo-classic mansion by Tresguerras, the architect of Celaya. It was built round a patio, the principal rooms being on the first floor. After some general conversation, and light but not unalcoholic refreshment, the lady of the house took us round. The rooms were high and rather empty, but extremely well kept. Some had modern furniture; others were more or less "period". Each room opened out of the one next it. The chapel had been dismantled and was used as a box-room, while bottles of Vermouth and other French drinks were standing on a ledge where an altar might once have been. This was the New Mexico, the Mexico of to-morrow; and the Governor's household were evidently setting the example that cleanliness should come before godliness. For the great attraction was the bath-room. It was built rather like an oratory; a pair of fluted columns and two steps led up to a bath like an altar, in cream and pink porcelain, with a shower like a *baldacchino*. At one side, instead of a stoup for holy water, there was one of those little basins you see in American pullmans, used only for cleaning teeth. Racks and pegs and brackets held the towels and tooth-brushes and tooth-mugs of the whole family.

In the late afternoon we went to a musical party at the house of a lady from Jamaica, married and settled in Guanajuato with a family already grown up. She spoke exquisite English —the first I had heard for some months—and played the piano rather well. It was a new baby grand; and one of our party, who is a professional pianist, was enchanted with it. She had not found a good piano since she left Europe, though her husband had found her a tolerable one to practise on, in Mexico City, by going to the *Monte*—not the "mountain", but the Government Pawnshop. There she sat, trying all the different effects of which a new and excellent piano is capable; and playing from memory Soler, Granados, Debussy, Ravel, Falla and all kinds of music to show her hostess how well the piano sounded. Then a married daughter of the house—a girl with something of the calm, exotic beauty of the bust of Nefer-titi at Berlin—danced in the costumes of different parts of Mexico, along with a Mexican friend of hers; a jolly tomboy of a girl, very Mexican and very Spanish and yet perfectly serious on one subject. She was engaged to a secretary of the Mexican Legation in Spain, which for more than two years had supported a colony of homeless Spanish children and was actually the last to leave the country before the advance of the Nationalists and their Italian allies. How ashamed I felt that that could not be said of the British Legation in Spain! But the things in Mexico which are good, and the people in Mexico who are serious, do frequently put an Englishman to shame nowadays.

The evening's lecture included some records of *cante hondo* from Seville sung by Niña de los peines; but I found them heart-breaking, impossible to listen to any more.

¡Esta luz de Sevilla!...La tierra de María Santísima. El Barrio de Santa Cruz. La Plaza de Doña Elvira. La casa de Rosina (del "Barbero") cuando era niña..., as Falla said.

Semana Santa. Tío Pepe. Saetas. Maestro Torres. "El Retablo de Maese Pedro."

The Dance of the Seises. Dancing to a barrel-organ with La — and La — (what on earth were their names?) in the Venta de Eritaña. That night club in the Calle de Amor de Dios, with its proprietor—shot, of course—who looked like a mission schoolmaster and was the only living disciple of Pí y Margall and the federal contract which was to be *sinalagmático, conmutativo y bilateral.*

Niña de los peines.

We know now what it all leads to. The occupation of Seville by foreign troops and a broadcasting general. What could *they* do with the incomparable art of Niña de los peines and the others?

> La Lola...
> la Trini, la Coquinera,
> la Pastora...
> y el Fillo, y el Lebrijano,
> y Curro Pabla, su hermano,
> Proita, Moya, Ramoncillo,
> Tobalo—inventor del polo—
> Silverio, Chacón, Manolo
> Torres, Juanelo, Maoliyo...
> Ni una ni uno
> —cantaora o cantaor—
> llenando toda la lista....

(Only stimulate their passions, perhaps, as so many other people did, as *cante hondo* always ended by doing....But passions like those!)

Someone, as Antonio Machado said, had sold the very stone of the household gods to the tedious Teuton, and the hungry Moor; and to the Italian, the very gates of the seas.

> Alguien vendió la piedra de los lares
> al pesado teutón, al hambre mora,
> y al ítalo las puertas de los mares.

Heart-breaking for Antonio Machado; heart-breaking for a mere foreigner as well.

The *Sevillanas* of Niña de los peines, which once would have excited me and disturbed me, were now unbearable. In fact they spoilt the evening for me—even the moonlight party, the *lunada*, on the edge of one of the reservoirs, given us by the Rector and served by Niña Chole and the Professor of Music. It might have been soothing, healing, if there had been no music louder than guitars; but though I am not an enemy of jazz, this occasion which might have been as wonderful and as memorable as another on which music for guitars was played beside the water in a garden at Granada, was spoilt for me by embittered memories of Spain and by one of the worst jazz bands I ever remember.

Chapter XIV

ALPHABETS FOR INDIANS

Not long after the lecture tour to Guanajuato, I was invited to take part in a congress of linguists and philologists. The main object of the congress was educational. Efforts to teach the large Indian population of Mexico to read Spanish had generally failed; but certain American scholars, working among the Indians, discovered that if an Indian was first taught to read his own native language, reading in Spanish would come much more easily. The Indian languages in Mexico are not merely an academic question; they constitute one of the most difficult social problems which the administration has to face. In Mexico there are something like fifty different languages, belonging to many different linguistic families. One of them—the modern form of the ancient Aztec—is spoken by nearly three-quarters of a million people; while three other, absolutely distinct, languages are spoken by about a quarter of a million people each.

The first duty of the congress, therefore, was to devise an alphabet which would suit all of the fifty-odd languages indigenous to Mexico, and yet be intelligible to country schoolmasters. The alphabet certainly looked complicated when the congress had done with it; but no individual language (and therefore no individual country schoolmaster) will have to cope with more than thirty letters, and some languages will need considerably less. Aztec, for instance (or its modern form, Náhuatl), has no *b, d, f, g, ñ, r* or *v*; and Maya no *d, f, g, r* or *ll*.

Some of the other languages are considerably more complicated. *Totonac* wants signs for seventeen consonants and seven vowels. *Mixtec* needs about the same number, with signs for the "tones"; for it is a "tone language", in something the way that Chinese is, and has three different levels of tone, or three different pitches. *Otomí*—one of the more important languages, spoken by a quarter of a million Indians in Central Mexico—needs signs for about twenty-two consonants and nine vowels, and it, too, has tones. *Tarascan* (though it has no tones) demands twenty-seven consonants and six vowels, with six more consonantal signs for the Spanish words which have been taken into the language. *Chinantec*, however, seems to require every possible device which linguists have ever invented. It has (I think) thirty consonant sounds, eleven vowels (all of which can be nasalized as well); three diphthongs, three different tones. Vowels can be long or short, but consonants can be long or short too. Further, it has the "glottal stop", and an effect called the "nasal inspiration"; and when spoken, it sounds—to me, at any rate—like a deaf mute trying to sell you a lottery ticket.

It may be imagined, then, that an order issued by the Mexican Ministry of Education—that country schoolmasters who did not speak the language of their district would be given three months to learn it, or be transferred to some other part of the country—caused considerable changes.

Choosing an alphabet was a long and complicated business. The idea was to provide a general, uniform alphabet from which signs could be selected to represent the sounds of the various Indian languages, and there was more than one way of approaching the problem. There was the scientific linguistic side: the unification of the various alphabets already used by linguists in scientific research on the various languages; and there was also the practical side: the formation of alphabets which should be adequate for writing the various languages for ordinary use. Further, there was the question of those languages which had already been reduced to writing, and had something that could be called a literature.

The congress had got together all the investigators of Mexican languages it could find. It had the warm support and encouragement of President Cárdenas; and was strengthened by the presence of some of the greatest authorities from the United States, as well as representatives from various Mexican Government departments and learned societies.

In Europe it is not generally realized, or only realized by specialists, how many Indian languages are still spoken in Mexico, and how many people speak them. The new Mexican census, to be taken in 1940, will certainly give a more accurate statement of the position than was possible when the last census was taken in 1930; but the extent of the main Indian languages in Mexico (out of a total population of some 16½ millions) is roughly as follows:

Náhuatl (i.e. Aztec)	680,000
Maya	235,000
Otomí ⎱ each Zapotec ⎰	220,000
Mixtec	170,000
Totonac ⎫ Mazatec ⎬ each Huaxtec ⎭	60,000
Tarascan	35,000
Chinantec	25,000

Besides these the assembly included investigators of four rarer languages: Popolac, Cuitlatec, Matlatzinca and Cuicatec, which seem to be dying out.

It may easily be imagined how serious a social problem is caused by the existence of so many Indian languages. According to the census returns of 1930 there were 2,251,086 individuals who spoke Indian languages, not counting 340,089 children less than five years old; that is to say, 2,591,175 or 16·65 per cent of the total population. Of these, 1,185,162 were "monolingual", i.e. speaking only one Indian language; while the "bilinguals", i.e. those speaking one Indian language and also Spanish, amounted to 1,064,234. Those who spoke two Indian languages were very few, only 1690. The importance of these facts cannot be overrated. They are not only of great interest to linguists, but have a considerable social significance. In the past, various methods have been used in dealing with the situation.[1] The first idea for the education of the Indians was to preach to them in Spanish or in Latin, though the multitudes who were forced to listen to such sermons knew no languages except their own. Then the Franciscans came upon the scene and set to work to learn the languages of the inhabitants: *la teología* (as one of them put it) *que de todo punto ignoró San Agustín*, a kind of theology of which St Augustine knew nothing. They began by devoting special attention to Aztec, which had been the language of the most important native state and was a kind of *lingua franca* over an immense stretch of country which began in the Mexican State of Sinaloa in the north and only ended in what is to-day the Republic of Nicaragua. Education was provided for boys, chosen from the more privileged classes among the Indians. Schools were first opened in Franciscan monasteries, where, in addition to religious teaching, lessons were given in those subjects which at that time constituted primary education, combined with practical instruction in arts and crafts. Teaching was given in the Aztec language; but at the same time the boys were taught to speak, read and write in Spanish.

In 1536 Bishop Zumárraga (afterwards first Archbishop of Mexico) noticed the ability of the Indian boys educated in this way, and decided to build a special college for them, where they could widen the scope of their studies and eventually become teachers themselves. So he founded the famous college of Santa Cruz de Tlaltelolco in the City of Mexico, with a staff of the best teachers available. The Indian pupils made great progress, while the more learned Spanish monks

[1] M. A. de Mendizábal, *Revista de Educación* (Mexico, November 1938), pp. 9 ff.

found that members of the college made excellent teachers of Indian languages—all the better for having had a good general education as well—and eventually they became the assistants and colleagues of those Spaniards who were engaged in linguistic studies. Some of them became compositors, making (as a rule) better typesetters than Spaniards; and before the end of the century the College of Tlaltelolco had a printing press, and issued important publications of its own. These (though mainly of a theological nature) served for the instruction of the Indians in their own languages, and were a prelude to the really memorable achievements of colonial philology, such as the great Tarascan dictionary of Gilberti and the few other philological works of the period which are still useful, and even indispensable, to modern scholars.

Yet the most important result of this system of teaching was not the production of capable assistants for the missionary work of the friars, but the great work of Bernardino de Sahagún, *Historia general de las cosas de Nueva España*— a general history of the institutions of New Spain. This was an ethnological and philological undertaking which even to-day is of the greatest scientific value; and if the plan of the book, the sifting and collation of the material, was due to the intellect of Sahagún and his vast knowledge of the Aztec language, the work was made possible by the help of members of the College of Santa Cruz de Tlaltelolco. Sahagún compiled a great part of his *Historia* in Aztec; and it is therefore a genuine expression of the real thought of the Mexican people at the time of the conquest, preserving in their own language their ideas of religion and ethics, and it serves as a basis for all modern research into the primitive customs and comparative religion, the legends and the poetry, of the original inhabitants of Mexico. Sahagún's book also includes something that has been described as the finest piece of literature of the American continent: the Aztec version of the Spanish conquest, which at times almost suggests scenes from the siege of Troy.

"It is difficult to imagine", says Professor Mendizábal, "what it would have meant to the culture of the peoples of America, if so wise and humanist a system of education had been allowed to go on through the four centuries of Spanish colonial administration and Mexican independence. The history of the Spanish American countries would have been very different, and their contribution to general culture far greater than that of the creoles and mestizos of to-day, with the almost total exclusion of the Indians, who, whenever they have risen to intellectual distinction, have done so as representatives of an adopted culture."

With the seventeenth century came a rapid moral and intellectual degeneration of the religious orders in Mexico. Sahagún's monumental work remained unpublished; while the commercial interests of Spaniards and creoles, planters, mine-owners and merchants, left no room for a creative and generous-minded institution like the College of Santa Cruz de Tlaltelolco, and had begun to undermine its influence even before the end of the sixteenth century. From that time onwards the culture of the Indians was completely neglected; and nothing further was done until 1921, when, under the administration of President Obregón, the first groups of lay missionaries were sent out by the Ministry of Education to travel through the length and breadth of the country and endeavour to arouse the Indians and agricultural labourers from the inertia of centuries. The teaching of Spanish had ceased to be in charge of men like Sahagún and his companions. They had been replaced by the bailiff of the *hacienda*, the *caporal* of the cattle ranch, the *capataz* of the mines, or whoever was in charge of the gangs of forced Indian labourers. All that it was necessary for an Indian to know of the language of Cervantes was enough to understand the word of command and to escape being flogged for disobedience.

The new system, introduced in 1921 for the Indians, was based on the principle of "incorporation", i.e. "bringing the Indians in". The object was to teach them Spanish at the same time that they were learning the lessons which correspond to the first four years of the elementary school.

The *misiones* generally failed. When it came to teaching an Indian to read, it proved almost impossible to get him to understand what the act of reading implied. First, the teacher might have to overcome the Indian's superstitious dread of a piece of paper with marks on it; such things contained a magic which might destroy his maize, his family and himself. Then there was the difficulty of making out the little black marks themselves. The marks (he was told) represented the sounds of a man speaking; but the man was not speaking the words which the Indian ordinarily heard and used in his own life, but words absolutely and entirely different—words only used by *mestizos* and foreigners. It was as if the reader of this book had not learnt to read, first of all, in English or Spanish or whatever was his mother tongue; but had had to do so in Arabic, Persian or Chinese—languages and writings full of ideas and ways of looking at things which were completely strange to him. Under such a system the Indian, whether monolingual or bilingual, went on thinking his own thoughts in his own language. Spanish was not a road to learning, but a barrier.

This was the crux of the problem. The population of Mexico which speaks Indian languages is increasing. The importance of knowing Spanish as well is obvious. So it is necessary to promote among the different Indian groups the widest possible knowledge of their respective languages; and yet not to neglect Spanish, which should be (as Aztec once was) the *lingua franca* for all the inhabitants of Mexico.

The congress was, therefore, faced with the task of providing elementary schoolmasters with an instrument—an alphabet—with which to carry out the ideas of the Ministry of Education, and change the present scheme of elementary education in Mexico, in so far as it concerned that part of the population which speaks Indian languages. There were several Indian delegates taking part in the congress. They were chiefly Aztecs and Zapotecs; and though the former were only distantly polite, as to strangers who could have no real knowledge of a subtle and expressive language like Aztec, the Zapotecs seemed to take a more human interest in the foreigners.

A fortunate reference to President Juárez (who was also a Zapotec), and my good luck in being able to read out, more or less intelligibly, a piece of the language written in the schoolmaster's own scheme of phonetics, completely broke the ice, and the Zapotecs and I met and parted on very friendly terms. Further, they went round to all the other Indian delegates, saying that the Englishman was completely impartial and had no axe to grind. Considering my ignorance of all the languages concerned (except Spanish) this was not far from the truth.

There were other Indians present, not so much as members of the congress, as to help in explaining and demonstrating any doubtful points that might arise in connection with the pronunciation of their own languages. There was a group of lively young Tarascans, and a Totonac boy who regarded the proceedings with unbounded amusement, especially the sounds of his own language, when he was called upon to demonstrate them; while at the inaugural meeting, a bevy of beauties from the Isthmus of Tehuantepec with their graceful carriage and superb national dress brought a splash of colour into what might otherwise have been a rather drab assembly.

The programme of the congress had been carefully pre-pared, and was well arranged with an eye to both linguistic research and practical application to teaching in an Indian language. The main object was to establish a general, uniform alphabet, from which could be selected the letters for the alphabets for particular languages. These alphabets were to be as simple as possible; that is to say, they should use only the signs that were found to be strictly necessary. There was to be the greatest possible uniformity between the several particular alphabets, so as to avoid difficulty and confusion, both typographical and phonetic, to students, teachers, employees and all who read native languages. The principle of "flexibility" was admitted, i.e. letters could be used in different senses in different languages provided that their values were similar and that such usage was possible or practical; while it was agreed that the alphabets should approach (as far as was practical in each language) as nearly as possible to the Spanish alphabet, so as to make it easier for an illiterate person to go from his own language to Spanish, which is, after all, the national language of Mexico.

Though the ideal to be aimed at was the principle of "one sound, one sign", the use of two letters to represent one sound was not absolutely ruled out, least of all when it was a case of bringing the spelling of a given Indian language into line with the spelling of Spanish. To insist, for instance, on a Greek lambda with a line through it to represent the familiar *tl* of Aztec, seemed mere pedantry. And—most important from the point of view of those who still find the act of reading trying and difficult, it was agreed to avoid "diacritic signs"—dots and dashes above or below the letters—as presenting difficulties alike to printers, teachers and writers. There is also the possibility that some of the Mexican languages may one day have to be transmitted by Morse, which makes the use of diacritic signs, as well as the principle of "one sound, one sign", quite impracticable.

The question of dialects—some of them mutually unintelligible—brought up several problems. One form of each language, one dialect, had to be taken as the "standard" language; and the standard language had to be chosen preferably from a dialect which had the advantage of being spoken by the group which was most important, culturally or numerically, and which included characteristics common to one or more other dialects. In the case of Aztec and Maya, the dialects chosen as the standard languages were those nearest to the forms spoken at the time of the Spanish conquest, and written down by Spanish investigators soon after. There is, as it happens, a large quantity of material, in manuscript and even in print, written in several of the Indian languages. The congress decided to set up an editorial commission to publish modern linguistic works which might be useful in the study of Indian languages; to collect and prepare such works for the press; and further to obtain funds for the purchase of the necessary founts of type, and to publish as soon as possible such works as were specified by the assembly.

The problem of rural education, specially dear to President Cárdenas and all Mexicans of good will, occupied a good deal of the attention of the congress. The great difficulty is to create confidence in the work of teaching people to read in native languages. This might be accomplished, it was thought, by making use preferably of country schoolmasters who were themselves Indians; of employing as masters Indians trained in the rural normal schools. It was no secret that a certain opposition to teaching the Indians to read their own languages comes from country schoolmasters who are not Indians; and while the official report of the congress does not say so, it was admitted that little but opposition was to be expected from the Church. As a practical point it was suggested that, in the beginning at any rate, only one type of lettering—of "lower-case" lettering—should be employed for reading-books, wall-sheets, the labels of gramophone records, notices, etc.; for anyone who has endeavoured, in middle life, to learn a language with an alphabet of its own and not the Roman alphabet (e.g. Arabic, Hebrew, Russian, or any British Indian language) will remember how different founts of type, or kinds of lithography, or even capital letters, seemed at one period to add to the difficulties.

The means of carrying out these plans were also discussed. The prime necessity was seen to be something on the lines of the *Misiones pedagógicas* which did such memorable and beneficent work in Spain. For Mexico, plans have been prepared for *Misiones alfabetizadoras*; and though a beginning is made in the native language of the district, Spanish is regarded as indispensable in any plan of education. Finally, there arose the question of how the study of native languages in Mexico was to be kept up. The congress recommended the foundation of a special Institute to deal with every aspect of the subject. This Institute has been called *Consejo de Lenguas Indígenas*, Council for Native Languages; its duties are to carry out studies on the structural and social aspects of native languages, contribute to the solution of problems of education in those languages and train investigators. It publishes a review and is forming a library; it is carrying out investigations into dialects which seem likely to disappear.

I must leave it to others to judge whether these results are adequate. The congress met every day for eight days, and sometimes for eight hours a day. The sittings were always long and sometimes arduous; but they were very interesting, not only linguistically, but psychologically as well. It often happened that when the clock had struck two in the afternoon, or nine in the evening, and the chairman was just going to adjourn the meeting for lunch or supper, an Indian (or one of the other delegates) would raise his hand and catch the chairman's eye. *¡Pido la palabra!* (*Je demande la parole*). Then we were in for another long, detailed piece of analysis, showing as often as not how something which had been proposed and very nearly agreed to, would not suit the particular language which the speaker represented. The representatives from the United States had come with a fully fledged "Americanist" alphabet of their own, an alphabet which is already in general use for the scientific study of North American Indian languages. This was compared with the European International Phonetic Alphabet, which seems to be sharing the fate of the League of Nations: everyone has got what they can out of it—particularly England and France —but no one supports it now. This is not the place to discuss whether the League of Nations was inadequate for America; but the International Phonetic Alphabet was certainly inadequate for North American languages. To take only the vowels and compare the two systems: the one can represent nineteen vowel sounds, the other thirty-one.

The alphabet for Mexican languages had, however, to keep where possible to the old Spanish forms, particularly with Aztec (which has a considerable written literature), and, to a less extent, with Mayan and Tarascan. I wish the congress could have given its alphabet a more Spanish appearance; and no one seemed ever to have heard of the Spanish modification of the International Phonetic Alphabet invented by Dr Navarro Tomás at the Centro de Estudios Históricos at Madrid, published in the *Revista de Filología Española* and (now that the members of the Centro are scattered over the whole of the Spanish-studying world) in use at the Instituto de Filología of Buenos Aires.

Though the congress in Mexico had not been informed of the fact, efforts not unlike their own to establish a standard alphabet had recently been made in Peru, where (as also in Bolivia and Ecuador) a large part of the population is ethnically and linguistically Indian. The alphabet adopted for Peru preserves the five Castilian vowels, adding two more, with the thirteen Spanish consonants and certain other signs to represent the characteristic sounds of the Indian languages concerned. The work of the Peruvian linguists was inspired (as was the linguistic congress in Mexico) by the work which North American linguists have undertaken under the "New Deal" of President Roosevelt, to educate the Indians in their own languages. The Peruvian alphabet has priority in Spanish America, although its results were unknown to the Mexican congress and were not published until some time after it had met. The fundamental object of the Peruvian commission (like that of the Mexican) was to unify and simplify the different ways of writing the native languages; and the alphabet proposed will replace the different systems which have been in use hitherto. Again, the Peruvian linguists, like the members of the congress in Mexico, tried as far as possible to make use of Spanish spelling, without doing violence to native phonetics.

The aims of philologists in both Peru and Mexico were, therefore, the same. It is not desirable that the Indians, by learning to read their own language, should be thereby isolated, or socially cut off from the rest of the population. For an Indian, knowledge of his own language should be a bridge to *castellanización* and the exchange or interpenetration of cultures in all the different ethnic sectors of the complex population of Spanish America.

There were (as I think I have said) several Indian members of our congress; and it was curious to hear from one of them some healthy anti-clerical sentiments. Propagandists in England would have us believe that such sentiments in Mexico would only be expressed by a "blue-chinned politician"; but here was an Indian—actually one of my friendly Zapotec schoolmasters—who obviously knew what he was talking about, and seemed only to be protesting at the centuries of oppression which his race had suffered. The congress was considering the philological work done in the past—particularly in the sixteenth and seventeenth centuries—by Catholic missionaries; and one of the delegates had explained in an admirably lucid discourse, which of those works still had philological value, and which had not. Then one of the two Zapotec delegates arose, and declared without mincing his words, that most of these monkish productions were made, not for learned purposes, but to convert the Indians to Catholicism; that in every sentence they sought to inculcate some religious teaching; while the Indians had a religion which, in the long run, was no more barbarous and bloodthirsty than that brought by the Spaniards, and had a moral code which was infinitely higher. This was exaggerated, but it wanted saying; yet it was said with such force, such conviction and such bitterness, that the chairman was obliged to call him to order and then suspend him; though most members of the congress, I think, really agreed with him.

Otherwise, my recollections of the congress are of a gathering which showed extraordinary patience and good temper, to say nothing of the devotion of some of its members who were obviously very busy men, and could ill spare the time that the sittings demanded. Next was the fact that everyone, without exception, addressed the congress in Spanish—even one highly gifted North American linguist who (it was said) had only been learning Spanish for about three weeks. The congress, it was felt, was being held in a Spanish-speaking country, and it was a matter of courtesy and good manners that Spanish should be the language spoken. The most learned of the younger linguists in the United States—as on other occasions in this book, I deliberately refrain from mentioning names—was often called upon to explain to the congress any doubtful points, and more particularly what the particular problem before us really was. He did so with a charming smile; and though he was often at the blackboard giving what was practically a lecture, his persuasive smile never left him. It was only when he sat down that his brow contracted and wrinkled, and then he looked like Beethoven. He had also a sense of humour, or of the humorous fitness of things. There was one moment when, to explain some point in the pronunciation of a Mexican language, he wrote on the blackboard certain phonetic signs which I deciphered as "weak worm". He added that the language was Mohican, and that the *k* might perhaps be written as a *g*. I began to get a glimmer of light; and when he said that the word meant a "house" I was sure. It was our very old friend "wig-wam", and in the Mohican language, too!

Chapter XV

Mexican Spanish

I felt rather an intruder at the congress of linguists which met to devise an alphabet for the fifty-odd Indian languages of Mexico. For though I had read a little of the grammar of some of them, I have no real knowledge of any, and merely looked through the pages of the grammars as one looks through a certain kind of novel—to see what happens and how it is done. "Have you ever *read* a grammar of Arabic—not learnt, but *read* one?" Sir Thomas Arnold asked, when I first went to him for elementary Arabic; and in the course of our studies he would suddenly ask: "Have you ever read a grammar of Chinese?" or "If you have ever read a Dutch Grammar, you will remember that the prepositions... whereas in Arabic it is very much simpler."

Sir Thomas was always right. Though one has to learn and memorize the grammar of any language one really takes seriously (the dummy Arabic verbs, for instance, or those public school Greek verbs, $\lambda \acute{v} \omega$ and the verbs in $-\mu\iota$) there is no reason against turning over the pages of the grammar of a language one will never have to learn; in fact, there is every reason in favour of it. So no one need be ashamed of browsing over the grammars of Mexican Indian languages without making any attempt to learn any of them. Students of languages are too easily frightened by the dread word "superficial". If a man or woman claims to be a trained linguist or philologist, it is different; there must be no superficiality about the languages one is really supposed to know: French, for instance, or Spanish, or our own language—English. But, for the rest, there is no harm in passing an idle hour with a strange grammar. If I lived in Mexico, I should take one of the Indian languages seriously—Tarascan, perhaps. As it is, the chief interest of a Spanish-speaking person visiting Mexico for a few months is to listen and hear what is happening to the Spanish language, and try to find out how far it is being affected by the various Indian languages by which it is surrounded.

Linguistic studies have become an extremely technical subject, with a jargon of their own. The use of jargon is justified, in this case, for it expresses exactly what the linguists mean; yet it should be possible to explain what they are getting at in plainer English, without being damned for superficiality. The writers who explain, as far as simple language will allow, what has been happening lately in mathematical physics, for example, are worthy of all respect and encouragement; and though it is clear that no one can hope to understand Einstein properly without learning the language of his mathematical formulae, it is possible, from the non-mathematical explanations which have been published, to obtain some idea of what he is getting at. Something of the kind is due in linguistics, and from my first week in Mexico I wanted to put down my impressions of the Spanish I heard, so that it should be interesting to my friends, particularly those who are not linguists.

But how could one do that for people who did not even know Spanish? It was a problem certainly. One way to begin was to see what Spanish-Americans themselves—and particularly Mexicans—had said about it, keeping one's ears open all the time for the Spanish that one heard spoken around one in Mexico. It so happened that just before I left England on my first visit to Mexico, I received as a present from the author a large and learned book on that very subject, *El Español en México, Los Estados Unidos y La América Central* (The Spanish Language in Mexico, the United States and Central America), by Dr Pedro Henríquez Ureña, published by the University of Buenos Aires. With a book like that to refer to there was nothing more to be done except keep one's ears open and listen to the Mexican voices around one. For Dr Henríquez has not only worked and published on the subject himself. In this volume he has reprinted everything of importance which has ever been written about Mexican Spanish by others, with footnotes of his own, saying whether he hears things in the same way as they do; and his collection of studies, and his remarks on them, are likely to be the last word on the matter for a good many years to come. They will be known already to specialists, but not perhaps to the more general readers (if there are any who have gone with me so far as this) in a book which is merely the account of a Spanish professor's sabbatical holiday in the New Spain.

On the whole, Dr Henríquez finds that what has happened to the Spanish language in Mexico is not so very different from what has happened to it elsewhere wherever Spanish is spoken, in Spain as in South America, in the Philippine Islands and among the Jews of Eastern Europe and North Africa. But in Mexico there are certain peculiarities which are found nowhere else.

What gives special character to the Spanish of Mexico is the survival of Náhuatl, the modern form of the old Aztec language, which has had a considerable effect on the vocabulary, and at times on the pronunciation of Mexican Spanish. Aztec was an agglutinative language, and ran to very long words; and words of Aztec origin are especially numerous in the Spanish of the Central Plateau, the Valley of Mexico. In Mexico City one finds the menu, for instance, full of Aztec dishes, and trams and buses going to places with Aztec names. There are various dictionaries of *Aztequismos*, but they have probably not yet collected all the aztecisms there are; Ramos Duarte notes 400 and Mendoza 900.

Nothing shows more clearly the dominating power of the Náhuatl language than the merely local position to which it has reduced the words in Mexican Spanish derived from other

Indian languages; for while Náhuatl has imposed its vocabulary over the whole territory of the old viceroyalty of New Spain and extends it to Central America, not counting such Aztecisms as those which now belong to the whole world—"cocoa", "chocolate", "tomato"—there are very few indigenous words from other Mexican languages which have succeeded in crossing the borders of their own districts. From Otomí, for instance, a "tone" language which shares with Náhuatl the greatest area on the Central Plateau, not a word reaches the educated classes and people who can read and write. Spanish words derived from Otomí do not get beyond country speech, or at most reach the markets of country towns. Ramos Duarte gives Otomí-Spanish words for "broom", "bucket", "lantern", "old woman", "itch", "drizzle" (*gwišmiš*, a word which conveys the idea of the sound of fine rain and the slush it produces), "mushroom", "Indian", "vulture", "sweet", and "drunk". These are only heard in the States of Hidalgo, Mexico and Tlaxcala.

Words from Maya, the dominant language in the peninsula of Yucatán, only reach as far as the neighbouring States of Campeche, Tabasco and Chiapas. An exception might be made for *henequén* (sisal hemp)—the most important produce of the peninsula—if it is a Maya word at all. It was already known in the sixteenth century to Padre Las Casas in the form *nequen*, and it may have come from one of the West Indian Islands, or be a loan word from Yucatán to one of those islands. In the same way the word *huracán* (hurricane) originally came from the Quiché language, and then became a loan word from Yucatán to the islands.

From the Tarascan language of the State of Michoacán comes a familiar Mexican word for "sandal" (*huarache*), and the names of various fresh-water fishes and fruits. The *Geografía del Estado de Michoacán*, by J. Romero Flores (1931), gives the Tarascan-Spanish names of several more fruits and berries, and a word used for dry pine-needles. But these can hardly be said to have passed into Mexican

Spanish, any more than the Tarascan names of trees and flowers, given in the *Catálogo de plantas Mexicanas*, by Maximino Martínez (1937) or in *Hoofways into Hot Country* by Marian Storm (1939).

Words from the Zapotec and Mixtec languages are confined to the State of Oaxaca. Zapotec words for "crab", "owl", "iguana", and "frog" have passed into the Spanish spoken locally, and Mixtec words signifying "woman", "basket", and "bumble bee"; while those from the Huaxteca language (of the States of Veracruz and San Luis Potosí) as well as the North Mexican languages—Cahita, Yaqui and Tarahumara —are confined to the State in which the Indians speaking them are found. In New Mexico there are hardly any indigenous words of local origin; Dr Espinosa heard only four, but he collected seventy-five Aztecisms.

The ancient Aztec language had a very large vocabulary, and its richness influenced the already rich vocabulary of Mexican Spanish, which is said to use a larger number of words than the Spanish in any other part of America. It is not only a case of the number of words. There is the power of expressing fine shades of meaning, the habit of distinguishing things and separating one thing from another (specially seen in the names of plants), the passion for making divisions and subdivisions; and it is not going too far to attribute these qualities to a survival of the mental habits and cultural traditions of the Aztecs in contact with the higher, Spanish culture of the towns in the times of the Viceroys. In any case, the Náhuatl language comprised a considerable collection of words; and, owing to its agglutinative construction, had the power of forming any number of new ones. Molina, in the sixteenth century, included in his *Vocabulario* 29,000, while Mendoza, in the nineteenth century, found more than 70,000.

Then there comes the question of accent, of intonation. In the popular speech of Central Mexico, the prevailing intonation is Indian. The melodic curves of spoken Spanish —whether heard by a musical ear in the street or recorded on a smoked, revolving drum in the laboratory—are practically the same as they are in Náhuatl; and, above all, they show the curious and characteristic final cadence. These curves gradually change as the speakers rise in the cultural scale; and on reaching groups which may be described as educated, the intonation of word and phrase is very different from what it is in more popular circles, though, even so, it has a distinct Mexican air. Dr Ignacio Alcocer, in his little book on the Spanish spoken in Mexico (*El Español que se habla en México,* 1936) puts it in this way:

The Indians, when they begin to speak Spanish, apply to it the prosody of their mother tongue, lengthening the vowels and putting into them the characteristic "sob" or "groan". This seems to us Mexicans to be the origin of the special sing-song, whining accent with which the Mexicans of certain districts speak Spanish. At times a man almost seems to sing it, or groans plaintively at you; while on occasions he will stop suddenly, as if he had received a violent blow in the stomach. From this comes the characteristic accent of the Mexican speaking Spanish, an accent very different from those which have become stylized in the different provinces of Spain.

Mexican Spanish has other features which have come to it from Náhuatl: "phonemes" such as *tl, sh* and *tz,* which a Mexican can pronounce without effort but which give considerable trouble to a Spaniard who has just come to the country. In the earlier days of the Spanish conquest, the Aztec words taken over by the Spaniards underwent many strange transformations. Apart from the curious approximations to the native names made by Cortés in his letters to Charles V, and by Gómara, by Bernal Díaz, and the other *conquistadores* who wrote of their experiences, the Aztec words taken into Spanish tended at first to be more hispanized, more Spanish in appearance, than they are to-day. This is not due to erudition—to the process which, in Renaissance times in Europe, gave many Latin words, in Spanish and English, a more Latin look in their spelling than their actual pronunciation demanded. In Mexico the original forms have been preserved, and are now returning, thanks to the large indigenous population which has preserved the old language. There has also been the influence of linguistic studies which aim at spelling the native words in the form in which they are generally pronounced.

The *tl*, for instance, had been converted into *t* or *cl*, while at the end of a word it had changed into *t* or *l*, or had disappeared altogether. Take *tlapanco*, the space between the ceiling of this room, where I am sitting now, and the roof over it. The little dictionary *México Nuevo* (1938) spells it *tapanco*; but Porfiria (who cleans up and makes the bed, and incidentally comes from Tlalpam) pronounced it quite clearly *tlapanco*. Again there is *metate* (*metatli*), the stone mortar in which I heard them grinding maize next door, before they started slapping it from one hand to the other to make *tortillas*. *Suchil* is a small tree or the flower of a *Hibiscus*, and (in combination) the names of various flowers such as *Suchicopal*, *Suchilcahue*. But it is now more usually heard in its original form *xóchitl* (*šočitl*), as in *atzcalxóchitl* ("ant flower", a zephyranthus lily with pink blossoms), *tlalcoxóchitl* ("flower in earth"), *Houstonia*; and *zempaxúchitl* (or *zempoalxóchitl*, "twenty flowers"), the Aztec marigold, the subject of a charming essay by the Mexican writer Guillermo Jiménez, where he spells it *cempasúchil*. Another word in which the *tl* is coming back is *cacle* (*cactli*), the rough leather sandal worn by country people.

The *tl* has survived in innumerable place-names: *Tlaxcala*, *Tlalnepantla*, *Tlalpam*, *Tlacotalpan*, *Cautla*, *Popotla*, *Cautitlán*, and especially in those ending with the locative suffix, *tlan*, meaning "place of". There is also the curious hybrid word *tlapalería*, seen over so many shops in Mexico City and other Mexican towns. It is derived (with a Spanish termination) from an Aztec word *tlapalli*, meaning "colour for painting", and implies the sort of shop called in England "artist's colourman", and so "ironmongery". In other words, the *tl* has reappeared after having dropped out for many years, as in *tetzontle* (the pink pumice stone used for some of the finest colonial buildings) which has been spelled *tezoncle* and *tezontle*; *paxtle* (the "Spanish moss", or *heno*, hanging parasitically from the branches of trees in Florida and other Southern States, and in Mexico in the woods of Chapultepec, and pronounced *pastle* and also *pascle*); *chilpotle* (or *chilpocle*), one of the most usual pepper plants (*Capsicum annuum*); and in the familiar *Popocatépetl*, at one time *Popocatépec*. It might seem curious that *Popoca-tépetl*, the "Smoking Mountain", should have returned to its original spelling while *Chapul-tepec*, "Grasshopper Mountain", should not; but in the latter the final *c* is a "postposition" (i.e. a preposition which is tacked on at the end of a word, instead of coming in front of it), and signifies "in", while this *tl* has dropped out according to the principles of Aztec word formation. The Aztec *tl* has even got into some perfectly good Castilian words like *almizcle* ("musk") and *alpiste* ("canary grass"), which Mexicans have pronounced and spelt *almistle* and *alpistle*.

The sound *sh*, or *š* (written *x*) was preserved in Mexican Spanish, as in Castilian, during the sixteenth century and part of the seventeenth. The author of *Don Quixote* would have pronounced it *kišote*, and the Italian spelling, *Chisciotte*, preserves the original pronunciation. In the seventeenth century the *sh* turned into *s*, or the Spanish *j*, or the Spanish *ch*. The floating gardens of Xochimilco (*sochi-milli-co*, "in the flower seeding-place") are now pronounced with an *s* at the beginning; and Mexico (originally pronounced *Mešico*) is now called *Méjico*, with the Spanish *j*, though still written Mexico.

The Aztec sound *tz* was transcribed by the Spaniards first as *tz* and then as *ç* (which letter was still pronounced approximately like *ts* in the sixteenth century). The termination *-tzinco*, for instance, became *-cingo*; we get it in the name of the monastery on the way to Puebla, which, spelled accurately, should be *Huejo-tzin-co* (*wešotl*, "willow"; *-tzintli*, a diminutive; *-co*, "in"). In the name *Malinche* (the nearest the Aztecs could get to Doña Marina, the secretary and interpreter of Cortés, and, nowadays, the mountain named after her), the *tz* of *Malintzin* has been converted into *ch*. In modern times *tz* is generally pronounced *s*; though it is still heard as *ts* in some familiar place-names—the Lake of Pátzcuaro; and the destination of a line of motor-buses in Mexico City, *Atzcapotzalco* (*azcatl*, "ant"; *putzalli*, "heap"; -*co*, "in").

The Spanish conquest caused the imposition of one culture upon several others; it mutilated the native cultures but could not suppress them altogether. This is to be seen in architecture, pottery, and popular textiles; it is also reflected in the language. But it would be quite wrong to say that all the peculiarities of Mexican Spanish were due to the influence of native languages. Of all the Spanish-American capitals, Mexico was the one which from the earliest times reached the greatest social and literary importance, not only for its wealth, but for the University (founded as early as 1535), and for the colleges in which were educated many men who were afterwards distinguished in learning and letters. There was, in fact, a cultivated society, to whose manner of speaking the most important people in the country endeavoured to conform; and it was this influence which was predominant in deciding vocabulary, phraseology and pronunciation. "If the Spaniards of Spain", it has been said, "had really preserved the Castilian language as it was spoken by Cervantes or Luis de León, they would have some justification for thinking that such changes in the language as have taken place in America were due to rustic manners and lack of education. But the evolution of a language is natural and inevitable, and the surprise caused in Spanish people by the peculiarities of American Spanish is no more reasonable than that felt by a Spanish American at the new words which are admitted every day in Castille." Both Spaniards and Spanish-Americans are aware that their manner of speaking is not the same; but that fact, rather than dividing them, makes them more interesting to one another. For after all, they both speak the same language; and both encounter the same sort of difficulties when they try to learn another, such as English or French. The differences between European Spanish and American Spanish, not only make people interesting to one another, but amusing. Even in Spain, no one looked down on anyone else because he had a provincial accent; he simply registered the fact that the man he was talking to came from such-and-such a province or district. The same is true for Spanish America. There is no question of snobbery; a man's speech may show where he comes from, but that is all. He may be speaking Spanish of a different kind, but it is still Spanish. What is more, it may be almost comic; yet as there is no trace of snobbery, so there is no trace of ridicule. A Spanish lady of my acquaintance was enchanted by the apparently naughty words used to her in private conversation (but in all innocence, as it seemed) by an extremely cultivated and charming Argentine woman friend; while the apparently harmless words which a European Spaniard must *not* use in Spanish America are, of course, a standing joke. (The same applies to a foreigner who has learnt his Spanish in Spain.) The absence of snobbery in questions of language is one of the great things which English-speaking people can learn from Spanish; an unusual form of speech or pronunciation should not have a social significance, but only a geographical one.

One of the commonplace assertions of writers—especially non-Spanish writers—dealing with American Spanish, is that the Spanish language reached America with many Andalusian characteristics. Such a statement is extremely risky, if not positively inaccurate. For one thing, the majority of the *conquistadores* and colonists were not Andalusians; and even if they had been, the differences in pronunciation which to-day separate Castilians and Andalusians, in the sixteenth century had not crystallized out. The coincidences (Dr Henríquez thinks) between Andalusian Spanish and the Spanish of America—frequent but far from general—are probably the result of parallel processes rather than influences.

The articulation of a word may be one thing in Castille and another in Andalusia; one thing on the high Mexican plateau and another in the islands of the West Indies; one thing in Buenos Aires and another in Lima. But all these variations, of which a great deal—and often rather too much—is made by writers who are not Spanish, have a common basis which distinguishes them at once from French or English.

There is no longer any doubt that, at times, the changes which have affected the phonetic system of Spanish have been produced independently in the same way in different places. An example is the diversity and complexity of the evolution of the sibilants. In the sixteenth century the Spanish of Castille lost three voiced consonants; *s, z* and (French) *j*, as well as the aspirated *h*. About the same time appeared the intradental articulation which is something like the English *th*, the *z* of modern Castilian, but it never reached Mexico.

Again, in the fifteenth century, there had already arisen the confusion between the two types of *b*, originally different in origin; and again, from the end of the seventeenth century, came the change of the Castilian double *ll* (as in "million") into *y*, a change which has not yet become general in the Spanish-speaking world, even in Andalusia or America. The difference between *ll* and *y*, Dr Henríquez Ureña found to be still noticeable in the mountain regions of Colombia, Ecuador, Peru and Bolivia; in Chile, in the north and south, but not in the centre; while in Mexico there is one enclave in the State of Morelos where the Castilian *ll* may still be heard. Orizaba goes to the opposite extreme, converting *ll* into a sound approximating to the French *j* (*ž*) as in Granada and elsewhere in the south of Spain, though *y* preserves the normal (and English) sound. Puebla, however, and Oaxaca, turn both *ll* and *y* into a French *j*, in much the same way as the Argentine does: instead of *caballo*, you hear *kabažo*; instead of *cigarillo, sigarižo*.

Mexico constitutes an historical unity, because the whole territory formed part of the viceroyalty of Nueva España, or came under its influence. In vocabulary, as already said, what gives character to the whole region is the abundance of words derived from Náhuatl; but in phonetics, the zone is not uniform. The principal region, both from the number of its inhabitants and the importance of its culture, is the high central Mexican plateau. In the speech of this region, Dr Henríquez found that not much breath is wasted in the emission of the sounds. It is not a very vigorous speech. The tempo is slow, but the pitch is rather high. The intonation, in the popular classes, is identical with that employed in speaking Náhuatl; but in the more cultivated classes the local accent is attenuated. The characteristic effect is the final cadence of the phrase, which is quite distinct from the cadence usual in Castille. In the Spanish of Madrid, a phrase of no particular emotional significance ending in a two-syllable word, describes a curve descending to the last syllable. From the last syllable but two to the last but one, the voice drops a sixth or even an octave; while from the last syllable but one to the last, the voice drops still further. The last syllable but one (though accented) is short; the last, long.

In the popular speech of Mexico, however, the voice rises about a third, from the last syllable but two to the last but one; and then drops a sixth from the last syllable but one to the last. The last but one is long; the last very short. (This, of course, only illustrates the general principle in a very rough way; the difference of pitch can be measured scientifically on a blackened revolving drum.)

Another feature of Mexican Spanish strikes the careful listener. Vowels tend to have a rather obscure, indistinct quality. The accented vowel is clear enough; but the unaccented vowels are short, and, when in typically "weak" positions—just before or just after the accented syllable—they tend to drop out and disappear. Thus *experimento* is apt to become *exprimento*; *policía, polcía*. Again, the final syllable is apt to be cut short by Mexican speakers, while in Spain it generally has its full value and in Castille is particularly broad.

In an announcement of the Tarascan dance of *los viejecitos*, the name came out as *viej-sits*; *puntos* became *punts*; *artes*, *arts*; *contentos, contents*; while such everyday phrases as *Pase usted* ("Come in") and *¿ Qué sucede?* ("What's the matter?" or "What's happening?") sound more like *Pas-sté* and *Qués-sede?*

Elision is common; and foreigners who omit to elide vowels which should be elided, are, if anything, more noticeable in Mexico than they were in Spain. Failure to do so is one of the commonest faults of non-Spanish people speaking Spanish, though it should be one of the easiest to remedy. In Mexico (as in Castille), they always say *d' este, d' ese, m' entiende, m' está*; when two similar vowels come together, one drops off. You also hear (as in many parts of Spain—only no teacher will ever tell you so) *tu 'stabas, aqui 'stá*. But in Mexico the process goes further. Practically the only form of the article before a vowel is *l*: *'l alto, 'l ancho, 'l agujero, 'l hacha, 'l agua, 'l ojo*, instead of *el*; *l' hora, l' única, l' agujeta* ("bootlace"), instead of *la*. You also hear *últim' hora, lo 'stán, qu' hicimos* (but *que hacemos*, as usual), *le dijo 'l compañero*. Another curious vowel effect is the pronunciation *páis* for *país*.

The consonants, as a rule, are very clearly articulated. There is a characteristic Mexican *s* (sometimes called "the Aztec *s*", although, strictly speaking, the Aztec language had no *s*). It is dental and made with the lower teeth; remarkable for its length. (It is not a hiss, like the Basque *s* in such a word as *vasco*, but is thicker.) It probably owes its character to the influence of Náhuatl, which, though it has no *s*, has three sibilants not unlike *s*—those which the older Spanish grammarians represented with *c, z, tz* or even *x*. Certain words, therefore, both indigenous and Spanish, have preserved the pronunciation of the English *sh* (*š*), which in the older Castilian was represented by *x*. In general, Mexican pronunciation, even among quite uneducated people, has no difficulty in sounding the consonants at the end of a syllable, *s*, *r*, *l*, *n*, as well as the typical Náhuatl *tl* and *tz*, which one hears in *Popoca-tépetl*, *Ixtac-cíhuatl*, *Azcapotzalco* (though sometimes *Ascoposalco*), *Miscoac*, *Chapultepec*, *Cuauhtémoc*, *Cuauhtemoctzín*—the last (in spite of recent efforts to the contrary) not being exactly a place of sound learning or clear articulation; it is, in fact, part of the "red-lamp" quarter of Mexico City.

Yet the fact remains that you hear all these names articulated with exemplary clearness. Even the *d* is maintained and carefully sounded in between two vowels, as in past participles in -*ado*—a thing which, so far as my experience and information goes, is not done in any other part of the Spanish-speaking world, even in Castille. There, past participles do not end in -*ado*, but in -*ao*, or (if you want to be very correct, in -*adho*); the *dh* (like the modern Greek δ) being equivalent to the *th* in "than", "then", "this", "those", "thus". The *d* in -*ado* is to be heard in the highlands of Colombia and Ecuador, and on the Mexican plateau. Dr Henríquez Ureña says that in a personal experience of eleven years, he never once heard -*ao* in Mexico City, except in a rapid phrase like *lo he comprao ayer* ("I bought it yesterday"). The man in the street says -*ado*, as anyone can hear; and I was sharply pulled up by a secretary, telephoning to remind me of an invitation, and hoping that it was not forgotten, *olvidado*. I must have answered in my (in this case) slipshod European pronunciation; for she replied, somewhat tartly, *De modo que usté no ha olvidado*, the consonants cutting like a knife.

The *d* in Mexico, then, so far from dropping, is reinforced. In the street you hear said with biting distinctness (at least, if the perpetual sound of motor-horns allows you to hear anything at all), *¡Ya se quedan parados!* ("now they've stopped"); or a woman saying emphatically, *¡Nada, nada!* ("nothing"). This firm *d* in between two vowels is one of the most striking things about Mexican Spanish, particularly in Mexico City itself. It weakens as you go up the social scale, and also as you travel north; it was not so noticeable at

Guanajuato as in Mexico City. Going north, too, the tempo of the language seems to get quicker (e.g. at San Luis Potosí), but the articulation of the consonants becomes less clear; while, on crossing the United States border into New Mexico, such Spanish as you hear is in complete contrast with that of Mexico City. "The tension is relaxed; the consonants are singularly weak, and often almost vanish altogether; while the intonation is of the Indian type."

The only consonant which sometimes drops out in Mexico City is *g*. Dr Henríquez has heard someone refer to her needle (*aguja*) without a *g*; and (as in parts of Spain) "water" (*agua*) becomes almost *áwa*; *antiguo*, *antíwo*. This, again (so far as its occurrence in Mexico is concerned), can be traced back to Náhuatl, which has no *g*. It is curious, however, that though *gu* before a vowel becomes *w*, an English word beginning with *w* will often be reinforced by a *g*. In the street I lived in, there was a statue of a man whose name was generally pronounced "Gwashington".

Mexican Spanish, of course, has no lisped sounds, as North Americans will be the first to tell you. They will rag you for your "Castilian Spanish" because your *c* and *z* sound (and should sound) something like the *th* in "thank", "theft", "think", "thaw", "thud"; while they will firmly pronounce the *c* and *z* like an English *s*. As a matter of fact, neither are right, neither they nor you; the English *s* is as far from the real sound heard in Mexico as the English *th* is from the sound heard in Castille.

The pronunciation, or mispronunciation, of consonants leads to the phenomenon which grammarians call "metathesis", but which to ordinary people in England savours of "Spoonerism". Metathesis, in fact, might be described as a Spoonerism with syllables instead of with words. Scientifically it is defined as the tendency to put two contiguous phonemes in the most comfortable order. There is a delightful story of Jean de Reszke and a pupil who was studying *Pagliacci*. *Io sono il progolo....* "No," said Jean, "not *progolo*, but

prologo!" "*Io sono il progolo.*" "Non, mon ami, *prologo.*"
And so on; a perfect example of metathesis, or (if you like)
"methatesis". This sort of thing happens not infrequently in
Mexican Spanish: *estógamo* (for *estómago*, "stomach");
redepente (for *de repente*, "suddenly"); *pader* (for *pared*,
"wall"); *sastifacción* (for *satisfacción*); *catredal* (for *catedral*);
while Porfirio Díaz was sometimes addressed as Don Profirio.
Calosfrío is usual among educated people for *escalofrío*
("shudder"); while *protocolo* can turn into *potrocolo*, making
the minutes of a meeting into something more like the tail of
a horse.

A phenomenon of much the same kind is "apocope",
which might be described as telescoping the syllables. A
familiar Spanish example is *Maritornes* (for *María Tornes*);
while in Mexico there were *Hernán* (*Hernando*) Cortés, and
Bernal (*Bernardo*) Díaz. In modern Mexico one hears many
conventional reductions of women's names: *Cata* (for *Cata-
lina*), *Ceno* (for *Cenobia*), *Espe* (for *Esperanza*), *Mari* and
Tere (for *María* and *Teresa*). These were also familiar in
Spain; but I had not heard *Meche* (for *Mercedes*) or *Chela*
(for *Angela*); while *Chole* (for *Soledad*) I had only met with
in the Niña Chole of Valle Inclán. The first Chole I met
belongs to a younger and more sensible generation. She is a
lawyer, though none the less attractive for that. Another
Chole I encountered was not devoid of attractiveness either;
there must be something fatal about this particular apocope.

The opposite process—adding a letter or a syllable, which
the word did not originally possess—occurs in the word for
"skirts", *enaguas*. The original form, belonging to the Island
of Santo Domingo, was *naguas*, which was treated by the
Spaniards as a feminine plural, *las naguas*. Among the
Indians of the West Indian Islands, *naguas* meant only one
very short skirt; but the Spaniards, in multiplying the word to
las naguas, also multiplied the number of *naguas* in the dress
of Spanish women, and ended by calling them *enaguas*, as if
they had something to do with being in the water (*en-aguas*).

The older Spanish form, *naguas,* dates from 1495; *enaguas* from 1524. Lope de Vega (who knew as much about skirts as any man, then or since) still called them *naguas*; Quevedo and others wrote *enaguas.* Finally in Mexico, a singular form was evolved—*enagua,* for "skirt"—though in popular poetry the form *naguas* is still heard for "skirts". *Y las naguas de percal,* Tata Nacho sings in one of his songs; and he also uses the archaic, but still Mexican form of the preterite, referred to on the next page.

The late Manuel G. Revilla, in his book *El Casticismo,* grouped what he called the "provincialisms of expression peculiar to Mexico" under seven heads. In the first came the names of things belonging to the country, which the Spaniards had never seen before and therefore had no words to express; animals and plants, food and drink, utensils and building materials. All these terms are, naturally, aztecisms. The second group contains words of Aztec origin, designating objects which have names in Castilian Spanish, but which in Mexico were known preferably by their Aztec names. There are also a few words of French and English origin; and Castilian words used in Mexico for objects which have other names in Castille. The fifth group includes some very interesting archaisms preserved in Mexico in current speech. The sixth, Spanish expressions which are peculiar to Mexico; and the seventh, those words which are generally mispronounced by uneducated people.

Some of these groups have already been mentioned. Interesting—and, for people who have lived in Spain, rather puzzling—are the Castilian words used in Mexico for things which, in Castille, are called something else. A bedroom, for instance, is not *alcoba* (our "alcove") as in Castille, but *recámara*; the tray on which morning coffee is brought is not *bandeja* but *charola*; *joven,* when used to call someone or attract his attention, is not patronizing (like the English "Young man!") but is practically equivalent to "Sir!" or "Mister!" *Chulo* and *chula* are more like "dear", or "pretty", than what they meant in Spain, which was something not very complimentary; one of the most offensive things that could be said of ex-King Alfonso was to refer to him as *el rey chulo*. Other familiar Mexican objects with unexpected Spanish names are: *chícharos* (instead of *guisantes*), "peas"; *frijoles* (for *judías*), "beans"; *saco* (for *americana*), "coat" or "jacket"; and a good many others, including *boleto* instead of *billete*, the ticket for a train and *entrada*, the ticket for a concert. Among the archaisms are the curious use of the old form of the preterite tense: *truje*, *trujo* (for *traje*, *trajo*), "I brought", "he brought"; while what are apparently neologisms are to be found in *chamaco*, "boy" (perhaps from the Aztec), and *amasía*, "mistress", or, in modern English "unmarried wife".

Of peculiarly Mexican phrases, two of the most curious are the uses of *mero* and *puro*. *Mero* has nothing to do with "mere"; it means "just", "exact". *Ya mero sale*, "he's just coming out"; *ahora mero* (or *merito*), "now at once", *el merito lugar* (N.B. the accentuation is *merito*, not *mérito*), "the very place"; or the grim phrase at the beginning ·of Mariano Azuela's well-known novel, *Los de abajo*: *¿Y porqué no le metiste el plomo mejor en la mera chapa?* ("And why didn't you give him the bullet right in his brain?"). Farther on in the same novel: *merito del ombligo*, "right on the navel". *Puro* is used in the sense of "only", *puramente*; and when a friend of ours, describing a meeting, remarked: *Éramos puras mujeres*, no moral question was involved, but merely the fact that only women were present. Another expression for "only" is *no más* (literally "no more"); *Ai tienes no más lo que me sucedió con él*, "I'm only telling you what happened to me with him". Other curious usages are *quesque* and *dizque*. *Quesque* is equivalent to *que dice que hay*: literally "What! you say that there are...", as in *Los de abajo* once more: *¡Quesque animales en el agua sin jervir! ¡Fuchi!* "What! You tell me there's animals in water that isn't boiled? Ugh!" In the same way, *Dizque* is equivalent to *dice* *que*; *izque* to *es que*. In Mexico, when a train or a person is late, you do not say *tarda*, but *dilata*; *ya no dilata*, "he won't be long now". *Ahorita* (literally "in a little now") means usually in about half an hour.

But what the hardened, seasoned traveller in Spanish countries most welcomes in Mexico is the softness and gentleness of most Mexican voices. One rarely hears a harsh or unpleasant word; "We talk", says Revilla, "in a tone that is rather muffled, almost in secret, and we are surprised and disgusted at the heightened tone which most strangers use in conversation." Those soft and gentle voices of Mexico! One of the things that I remember most!

Chapter XVI

THE NEW PILGRIM FATHERS

The congress on the Indian languages of Mexico has led me on to the peculiarities of Mexican Spanish. From that, it seems a natural step to the Spanish people themselves; not the Mexicans, but the Spanish *émigrés*. I use the word *émigré* because I cannot think of an English word which expresses the exact shade of meaning that I want; the difference between the Spanish *emigrante*, the person who leaves his country of his own free will, and *emigrado*, the man who goes because he must, and goes for political reasons. Modern usage has fixed on the word *refugiado*, refugee, which is unfortunate, and has still a somewhat derogatory implication, in Spanish as in English. The Pilgrim Fathers were more fortunate. What is more saintly than a pilgrim? What more respectable than a father? Whoever gave them that name has done more for their reputation than even Miles Standish. That, and the fact of their coming in a ship called the *Mayflower*. Our *Sinaia*, *Epanema*, *Mexique* cannot compete with a name like that; but the passengers they carried have, I think, every right to be called "New Pilgrim Fathers", and the first contingent actually travelled on a pilgrim ship. America has always been a refuge for those fleeing from religious and political persecution, and the Spanish Pilgrim Fathers were undoubtedly flying from both.

The *Sinaia* reached Veracruz on June 13th, 1939, with 1619 Spanish passengers: New Pilgrim Fathers. Their arrival was by far the most important thing that happened while I was in Mexico. It was the beginning of a planned immigration. Some writers consider that it may have, on a smaller scale, such social and cultural consequences as to make it comparable with the exodus of those highly civilized refugees from Constantinople, who spread over Europe teaching Greek and led the way to the New Learning. I should rather compare it to the movement of the Huguenots who came to England and America after the revocation of the Edict of Nantes, and became some of the best citizens that those countries have ever had.

The New Pilgrim Fathers were not the first Spaniards to reach Mexico, fleeing from the tyranny of Spain. Small groups of exiles had arrived earlier—the original members of the *Casa de España*, for instance, whom I had come to Mexico to visit at the end of 1938; they had left Spain before the recognition of General Franco, and were not, therefore, technically refugees. There was also a large and efficiently run colony of Spanish children at Morelia, some of whom have since been adopted and given homes by kindly Mexicans in other places. The members of the *Casa de España* were all well-known scholars or men of science, and, as such, welcomed without question by the Mexican Government. But of those on the *Sinaia*, only about 200 were classified as intellectuals. The majority were skilled workers and farmers, carefully selected by the immigration service and approved by the Mexican Minister in Paris.

On board the *Sinaia* was the wife of a Mexican painter, who is herself Professor of Mexican Literature at the National University. She had done notable work to mitigate the sufferings of Spaniards in France, and was now charged with an official mission from the Mexican Legation in Paris to the Spanish *émigrés*.

"We had hardly left France", she told a Mexican reporter at Veracruz, "when I had a conversation with several passengers travelling on the *Sinaia* to see how we could arrange to give the other *émigrés* some sort of introduction to the country to which they were going. I lent them all the books of reference they needed to prepare talks on Mexican life, geography, history, literature, painting, music and social conditions. These talks were meant to rouse interest in every aspect of the Mexico of to-day. Needless to say, they were a striking success. The Spaniards who came on the *Sinaia* were most anxious to hear about the new Spanish-speaking country which henceforth was to be their home."

Other activities on board included the publication of a newspaper, and the formation of a card index of the occupations, trades and professions of all the passengers, with their past history and grade of technical and professional attainment. It is a record which has proved of great value in the distribution of passengers to employment in different parts of Mexico. "Of course", she added, "there were festivals on board; balls, *verbenas*, regional dances, *tertulias*; and I could see how all the passengers preserved their national characteristics, their 'complete and imperishable Spanishness', their *integra e imperecedera españolidad.*" This feeling of nationality will undoubtedly be preserved by them in Mexico, and will be a means of keeping their ideal vividly before them. "The spirit of the Spanish people is not dead. On the contrary, the momentary success of foreign aggression has caused this spirit to rise to greater heights than before. Face to face with destiny, the morale of this people is invincible; and for that reason it will triumph in the end."

The New Pilgrim Fathers had a wonderful reception in Veracruz. President Cárdenas would have come himself, if he had not been in the extreme north of the country, inspecting personally what was being done to improve the hard life of Mexicans in the hot deserts of Sonora and Lower California. However, he sent to Veracruz a personal representative, who, in a rousing speech, told the newcomers that Mexico was delighted to welcome immigrants from Spain.

The Minister of the Interior was more explicit. With the arrival of the *Sinaia* (he said) it seemed as if the misunderstanding of centuries had been ended. They were not being received as outcasts, objects of charity; they were the warlike defenders of a democracy which had striven against a world-wide totalitarian conspiracy. The Government and people of Mexico welcomed them as the defenders of liberty. They were received as brothers because they came to Mexico to go on with their work in peace. They were returning to the home founded by their ancestors, to a place where they spoke the same language, to cultivate the land, to develop industry, bringing new economic resources, technical capacity and strength to labour. The other values which they represented in science and letters would contribute to the light of national culture in Mexico, and the Mexican people would profit by the example of Spanish intellectual life, which had put all its resources at the service of the Republic.

In the capital there was general sympathy, apart from those individuals who got all their ideas from the reactionary evening papers. Mexico is a free country, and decent citizens were proud to welcome the New Pilgrim Fathers. The problem of settlement was dealt with at first by the Mexican Immigration Department and a Technical Reception Committee. It was decided to take one family into every *ejido* (communal farm), estimating the total possible at 40,000. The Trade Unions immediately made the immigrants members of the unions equivalent to those to which they had belonged in Spain. They pledged themselves to find work for the refugees and, until it was found, guarantee them food, lodging and a minimum wage.

Delegates and telegrams from all over Mexico reached Trade Union Headquarters at Veracruz, asking for the privilege of entertaining Spaniards. The acceptance of Spanish exiles in Mexico depended in the first place on the extent of persecution and danger to which they had been exposed. The number eventually to be admitted was to depend on the resources at the disposal of the reception committee, so that their coming to Mexico should contribute to the economic and cultural development of the country and prevent them becoming a charge on public funds. As far as political activities were concerned—a point to which the Mexican evening papers were always returning—it was stated categorically that Spanish immigrants would have the same rights as other aliens residing in Mexico, and the same obligations. The most convenient agent for their accommodation was first found in Dr Negrín, ex-premier of the Spanish Republic. Later, he was succeeded by Indalecio Prieto.

The Mexican arrangements were as good as the complicated nature of the problem would permit. Methods of distribution to different parts of the country were worked out; assistance was provided for refugees and their families; instructions were issued alike to labour organizations and to Governors of States, to give every kind of co-operation and help, by doing everything they could to help the Spanish immigrants.

But Mexico is not only a free country. It has a free press, and the totalitarian countries and their agents in America have not been slow to take advantage of the fact. In Mexico City, half the morning papers and all the evening ones are against the democratic countries. These papers have the largest circulation in the capital and the widest distribution in the provinces; while the news they publish from Europe shows quite clearly (to anyone who lives in Europe) that it originates in the "hand-outs" supplied by the propaganda offices of Dr Goebbels and his opposite number in Italy. Some of them are in close touch with the German Legation. It was obvious, then, in Mexico, that something would be done by these anti-democratic and so-called "Independent" groups to profit by the occasion, and use the presence of Spanish immigrants as ammunition against the Cardenists in the 1940 presidential election. A lead has already been given by the Right-Wing press in France; while in England the supporters of General Franco were doing all they could to blacken—or redden—the character of the Spaniards.

In Mexico, the landing of the Spanish immigrants became a question of party politics. The situation was complicated by the fact that there were numbers of Spaniards already in the country. Some had reached Mexico during the war, and were by that time involved in reactionary politics against the Mexican Government; while the Nationalist Spanish "agent" had somehow managed to become a naturalized Mexican citizen. Other active sympathizers with General Franco were drawn from the ranks of the Gachupines.

The Gachupines were naturally opposed to any immigration of Spanish Liberals. They would have preferred Fascists or monarchists, and their Mexican friends would too. They could come to terms with men like that, if indeed they had not done so already, as their predecessors had in the days of Iturbide, Juárez, Maximilian and Victoriano Huerta; and they were warmly supported in their protests by those Mexicans, who, since the days of Porfirio Díaz, had lost their properties and privileges and saw a chance of getting them back again. So the Gachupines played on the fear and egoism of the "independent" Mexicans who were against the Government, to stir up ill-feeling against the Spanish *émigrés*.

About this time a Right-Wing candidate appeared for the presidential election: a millionaire general, whose cause (*The Tablet* said, on September 7th, 1940) was "both the cause of the Church and of British and American oil interests". He was in fact a man of integrity, popular in many quarters, with personal qualifications of a very high order. As a method of attempting to discredit the administration of President Cárdenas, the so-called independent parties began another offensive against the Spanish refugees, who naturally were not in a position to defend themselves.

President Cárdenas, on his return from his long progress through the Northern States of Mexico, spoke with unaccustomed severity of the campaign of slander and provocation carried on against the Spaniards. There was (he said) nothing whatever to justify it. The Spanish immigrants came as workers, not as politicians, and did not turn any Mexicans out of their jobs. The agitation made by certain sections of the press over the arrival of the Spanish exiles was typical of the unrest artificially fostered in Mexico; there was no excuse for it. Everyone knew that Mexico needed more population. With that object, something like a million Mexican workers had been repatriated from the United States. Yet there was still room for large contingents of healthy immigrants; and none were so appropriate as the Spanish, who were, after all, of the same race; for most Mexicans are descended one way or another from Spaniards. It was quite untrue that the refugees came to form assault troops in Mexico. Apart from reasons of humanity (which even in the barbarous modern world still have to be taken into consideration by decent countries), the establishment in Mexico of Spanish immigrants was beneficial to the Mexican people. They came (he repeated) as workers, not as political agitators. It was of little importance that they held to the ideas which had kept them going in their own country; in Mexico they would merely get on with their jobs. Nor did they displace any Mexican from his work. All that had been asked for was co-operation between the organizations concerned, and that co-operation had been frankly and sincerely given. In those conditions several thousand refugees might be settled in Mexico; but the immigration would be limited by the possibilities of the country and what was most in keeping with its interests.

The observations of the President gave the commonsense view of the matter. After all, he was in a position to know what he was talking about, and to know rather better than anyone else. No one (certainly no other living Mexican) can have travelled over the country so widely as he has, or have heard the views of so many sorts and conditions of Mexican citizens. He has always been ready to listen to humble people who come to him with their difficulties and complaints, while his Indian connections assure him the sympathy of masses of the population who are quite unmoved by totalitarian rhetoric.

Immigration is one of the problems which have always existed in Mexico, but have seldom been approached in a scientific spirit or in the best interests of the country. Mexico includes large areas which have never been exploited—or even explored—as they might be; there may still be regions with unsuspected natural resources, while the comparatively small population is insufficient—and insufficiently trained, as a rule —to make the most of its great natural wealth. It is clear that Mexico needs immigration from abroad in order to be capable of a more complete economic development; and the problem has always been to find out which immigrants are the most suitable.

There are, it is considered, certain highly developed countries whose nationals would make useful and desirable immigrants for Mexico. But since those countries have overseas possessions and dominions of their own, it is unlikely that any large number of their subjects will find their way to Mexico, even if they could get accustomed to the somewhat different conditions and standards of life. On the other hand, the nationals of certain other countries which might send (and be glad to send) immigrants to Mexico, are for various reasons undesirable. Further, immigrants of distinct race which can only with difficulty be absorbed into the population of Mexico, would be, for many reasons, highly inconvenient. The ideal immigrants for Mexico would come from a country with close racial and cultural affinities, healthy and hardworking human stocks, and population to spare. The only country which fulfils all these conditions is Spain.

Before the Spanish war normal emigration to Mexico brought elements which were not always suitable; they were generally drawn from those who left Spain through professional incompetence, not being able to stand the competition of better workers in their own country, or for other reasons which need not be specified. It is not suggested that these elements were all undesirable, but simply that they did not represent the highest level of Spanish labour. It was obvious that a good workman or foreman who had been able to make a satisfactory living in Spain would not leave a condition of security to come and establish himself in an unknown country like Mexico.

The defeat of Republican Spain brought a complete change in the situation of those who might have gone to swell the ranks of Spanish immigrants in Mexico. Now for the first time it could be said that, among the contingents of immigrants from Spain, were many who in normal times would have gone on living and working in their own country. So that the occasion of General Franco's success gave Mexico the chance of large numbers of desirable immigrants, most of whom in the ordinary course would never have gone there at all.

Unfortunately, the Nazi invasion of Poland and the entry into the war of England and France have made it impossible for many more Spanish refugees to be conveyed to Mexico. The President had been willing to accept as many as 30,000; but the ships were no longer available, and thousands of men who would have made good Mexican citizens were left in concentration camps in France, sent to build roads or fortifications, or thrown on the clemency of Fascist Spain.

The total number of Spanish republicans who have reached Mexico is about 6000. *The New Republic* for September 27th, 1939, gave exact figures as they were at that date. Collective immigration: *Sinaia* 1620, *Epanema* 998, *Mexique* 2200. These, together with refugees who arrived on other ships in smaller numbers, bring the total up to 5618. This (as the writer remarks) should dispose of the tendentious statement that fifteen or twenty-five thousand "red soldiers" came to Mexico. "There are soldiers among these men, of course, some hundreds of ex-soldiers of the Spanish Republic. But there are also a large number of civilians, including intellectuals, women and children. There are 1460 unmarried men and 45 unmarried women. There are 685 refugees less than fifteen years of age. There are 496 men registered as intellectuals, 782 registered as factory workers, 706 registered as agricultural workers and 276 who are carried on the books as without profession."

Out of the 706 agricultural labourers who came over, 600 were reported in September 1939 to be working on the land

in various parts of Mexico. A large *hacienda* has been bought
in the North Mexican State of Chihuahua, on which, it was
hoped, 1200 Spanish families could be settled. Two smaller
haciendas were also acquired in the state of Michoacán, and
factories were started in other places.

"Mexico", an American newspaper observed, "is the only
country that has opened her doors more or less freely to the
Spanish Republicans. Chile accepts some immigration, but carefully selected by profession. Cuba has also accepted a few; Santo
Domingo within the limits of its possibilities has been very
generous.... If there are people who relate the present to the past,
and both to a possible future, the refugees who have come to
Mexico will not be wholly forgotten in the overwhelming disasters
of the day. While Europe plunges on to the ruin which might so
easily have been avoided a year or so ago—the ruin which the
Spanish Republic fought to avert—these victims of the monstrous
policies of 1938 are left to contemplate, from their misery and
exile, the exact results which they foresaw and which they did their
utmost to ward off from a threatened world."

Repercussions of events in Europe may be felt in Mexico
too. "Things are looking very ugly", the lady of the house
remarked. She had had a long life and remembered many
things. She had been one of three little girls chosen to offer
a wreath to President Juárez when he drove into Mexico City
after the retirement of the French and the capture of Maximilian; and, being the tallest, had been told to put it over his
head. But either her nervousness, or the President's ugliness,
had made her get it the wrong way round, so that the strings
hung down in front of his face, and he looked uglier than
ever, and extremely comic.

"Things are looking very ugly": *las cosas están poniéndose
muy feas.*

They will get uglier still, if the strife which certain foreign
interests in Mexico are endeavouring to stir up should break
out in another civil war; but we shall know where the blame
really lies. It will not be the fault of President Cárdenas, or
the Spanish Pilgrim Fathers.

Chapter XVII

Mixed Memories

Two visits to Mexico, one of sixteen days and the other of six months, have been enough to convince me of one great fact which I had never suspected; that Mexico is one of the most beautiful countries I have ever seen—and I have been in most countries in Europe. No book has ever done justice to the beauty of Mexico, and perhaps no book ever will—least of all this humble effort of my own, left unfinished and without the last touches which I had hoped to give it. If only there had been no European war! But the causes and the might-have-beens are now subjects for the historian, no less than the causes and might-have-beens of the wars in Spain and Mexico. For, if it is true of Spain (as Ortega y Gasset once said), that it is a country of infinite possibilities which have hardly ever been realized, much the same is true of Mexico. The great cause which has kept modern Mexico from realizing its full possibilities is—*war*.

It may be said of Mexico, as it was once said of Ireland, that there are a great many lies told about the country, which are not true. So far as most English writers have been concerned—English writers, but not generally Americans—Mexico has been interesting only for two reasons: oil and persecution. The oil is certainly there, in the subsoil; and the Mexicans claim that it belongs to them, though they would probably admit that the machinery still belongs to the foreign companies. It would be impertinent for me to suggest that it might be possible to reach a settlement on these lines; I leave that to Mr R. H. K. Marett and those who have made a study of the subject, remembering the remark made to me by a Mexican (very much involved in oil, at that moment) at a Christmas party, that oil need not affect cultural relations. As to religious persecution, it is (so far as my experience goes, and so far as I have been able to find out by inquiry) mostly imaginary. I know that priests are not allowed to wear their soutanes in the street, or appear in public in what I once heard Dr Inge describe as "the grotesque habiliments of a dignitary of the Church". But that restriction is not a piece of persecution, deliberately invented by a "godless and bolshevistic" Government in modern times; it goes back at least as far as the golden age of Porfirio Díaz. Evidence may be found in the great travel book by the late Dr Gadow, of Cambridge, *In Southern Mexico*, published as long ago as 1908.[1]

I had meant to use Gadow only as a witness to the beauty of Mexico, and more particularly, to its marvellous vegetation; but the legend of religious persecution in Mexico dies hard, and it may be worth quoting Gadow, a trained scientific observer, on what he saw in the good old days of Porfirio Díaz. On p. 453 he notes that the whole of the Mexican Republic enjoys now (1908) absolute freedom of creed. The Church was disestablished: Church buildings belonged to the State. Religion was—rightly, he thought—considered a private affair, and on no account to be used for political purposes. Hence religious processions were prohibited outside the churches; while within, full freedom and the safety of the articles contained in the inventory were guaranteed by the State. This was (and is now) enforced so strictly that no priest might appear in public in his official vestments. It might be pointed out once more that this was the condition of things under the administration of Don Porfirio, to which modern clericals and the "independent opposition" now look back as to a golden age.

[1] See also G. Baez Camargo and Kenneth G. Grubb, *Religion in the Republic of Mexico* (1935).

Another question which I had meant to avoid, but am always being asked, is whether the Government of Mexico is not "red". The answer is an emphatic "No". It has no connexion with Soviet Russia, and has for several years had no diplomatic relations with the Soviet Government. The Mexican Government is sometimes called Communist, and sometimes Fascist. The truth is that it is neither. It is not dictatorial. It allows a far-reaching freedom of discussion and tolerates a venomous and unscrupulous political opposition. The Government of President Cárdenas stands to the Left. It is Trade Union and Liberal-Socialist; supported mainly by the unions and also by the army.

Meanwhile the opposition is not merely tolerated, but is lively and active, above all in business circles in Mexico City and Monterrey. It is, of course, the duty of an opposition to oppose; but the idea that a parliamentary opposition should also co-operate is quite foreign to Mexican politics; and young Mexicans of Right-Wing tendencies, educated at Beaumont and Stonyhurst, have never heard of the phrase (or the idea—a fundamental idea in the Constitution of Great Britain): His Majesty's loyal opposition. In Mexico, several of the big opposition newspapers—and (as I have already pointed out) half the morning papers, and all the evening ones, belong to the opposition—receive news (and, it is said, subsidies) from German and Italian sources and so serve the ends of totalitarian propaganda; while these mouthpieces of the opposition at the same time declare that they are democrats.

The future political development of Mexico will depend on the presidential election, held in the summer of 1940. Good observers consider that in no other American country is the separation between Left and Right so wide as in Mexico; though it can be said with certainty that the Left-Wing groups at present in power are in no way Communist, and leave expression of opinion a wide field, even to outspoken and uncompromising Fascists; though the opposition is not for the most part Fascist either.

Socially, Mexico seems to have a curious and striking resemblance to the Spain of a hundred years ago, as described by Mariano de Larra. Writing in *El Español*, June 23rd, 1836, Larra declared that there were in Spain three distinct peoples:

(1) A multitude indifferent to everything, brutalized, and useless to the country for many years to come, because it had no needs and lacked all stimulus. Accustomed for centuries to yield to pressure from above, it could not move for itself but waited until it allowed itself to be moved by others. This (Larra observes) was useless, if not directly harmful; because the only influences capable of inducing animation were not always in the direction required.

(2) A middle class, which was gradually becoming more enlightened and beginning to have needs of its own. It was just discovering that it was in a bad way; that it wanted reforms, because change was the only way by which it might better itself. It was a class which saw the light, and already enjoyed it: but, like a child, it did not try to calculate how far away the light was. It believed things, when it wanted them, to be within reach if it stretched out its hands to take them; but it knew neither how to deal with light, nor in what the phenomenon of light consists, nor yet that light, when clutched with both hands, is apt to burn.

(3) Lastly, there was a privileged class, brought up in, and dazzled by, foreign parts; the victims (or children) of political emigration. It believed that it alone represented the country and was surprised at every step to see itself only a hundred yards in front of the rest. It was, in fact, a trotting horse, which thought it was harnessed to a "Tilbury", and then found that it was expected to drag a heavy covered waggon. So it rose on its hind legs, broke the traces, and went off on its own.

I have left this in the language and imagery of 1836; but even so, it seems so closely applicable to Mexico at the present day as to need no further explanation or comment. Not that Mexico is a hundred years behind Spain; far from it. Indeed the Old Spain, in its present condition, will take·many years to catch up the New. It is not for nothing that Mexico is in America.

Gadow's book has been so forgotten by recent writers on Mexico that there can be no harm in returning to it for evidence of another most characteristic aspect of modern Mexico: the survival of pagan cults in Catholic disguise. *Idols Behind Altars* is the title of a recent American book which deals with this subject; while more evidence is available in *Mexican Mosaic* by Rodney Gallop.

During his journey through Guerrero, Gadow saw and heard many things which threw unexpected light upon the natives' religious state of mind.

"It may not happen everywhere," he says, "the people take good care of that, but such things as the following do happen. The church, even in an out-of-the-way place, looks and is well kept; there are beadles and churchwardens and a choir, and when the bells are rung for the *oración*, vesper or curfew, the people take off their hats and cross themselves; some go to Mass, and they besprinkle themselves with the holy water, and they do all that and more. It is well to be on the safe side; and one can never tell what it may not be good for. But go inside, on a day in mid week. On the altar stand the customary images, etc.; the Madonna in front of the cross, before her a gaudy vase with withered flowers. On either side she is supported by the clay figures of native gods, also supplied with flowers. But these are fresh, and are put into the crown of the idol, which in reality is often shaped so as to serve as a flower vase. These 'idols' disappear towards the end of the week, when the padre is expected; they are put underneath the altar, or behind it, into a niche, and if the ecclesiastic is a zealous fool he finds them and makes a fuss, and then he cannot even get a 'niece' to cook his dinner. The worldly man states in his annual report that thanks to the enlightened and vigorous action of the local authorities, in harmonious work with the clergy, and through divine help, the last traces of heathenish idolatry seem to have disappeared—at least no case has come to his knowledge.... Only the Governor wonders what has come over his faithful heathens."

Writing this in America, while the gardens of my own country are reported ploughed up to plant potatoes, I cannot

but admire the "faithful heathens" in Mexico for their love
of flowers; and a clay figure of a native god which also serves
as a flower vase seems to be a distinctly happy invention.
Mr Desmond MacCarthy has remarked somewhere on the
propensity of people in England to have a makeshift garden
even in the most unpropitious places. Look at the sordid
backs and pinched front courts of small, grimy houses in our
towns! Foreigners (he added) have sometimes been surprised
that the English, of all people, should excel in poetry: "but
when I see in summer those little backyards blooming among
broken litter, dirt, and drying clothes, they suggest to me a
subsoil in which the English lyric genius has its root." Is it
an accident that the three most civilized peoples—and also the
three most democratic peoples, English, French and Dutch,
and their descendants in America—have been the greatest
cultivators of flowers? And war, the bringer of all ugliness,
which touches nothing without destroying or vulgarizing it,
makes us also destroy our gardens.

Mexicans—the Mexicans of to-day, at any rate—cannot
perhaps be called great gardeners, and the flowers they cultivate are as a rule less interesting than their wild flowers; but
both components which have gone to make the Mexican
people, Spanish and Indian, certainly have a passion for
flowers. One remembers those carnations in pots in some of
the humblest dwellings in Spain; the "Morning Glories"
trailing down from the window of a grimy tenement in
Mexico City; and above all, the passion—the religious passion
—of the Indians for growing, in old tin cans, anything which
has a bright blossom or a green leaf. A tumbledown shack in
the State of Veracruz had enough flowers and ferns in front
of it to have supplied several stands at a flower show. The
cans were battered and rusty, hanging from the roof, or
perched on any convenient ledge or projection; yet the flowers
were cared for, and the family seemed enormously pleased
that a mere stranger should take an interest in them too.

I said that the Indians had a "religious" passion for flowers, and the word was used deliberately. That has been so from the time of the Aztecs. Mrs Matchat gives several examples in her book, *Mexican Plants for American Gardens*, and a more modern case was described lately by a Mexican writer, Sr Guillermo Jiménez, in an essay "Las flores de Zapotlán".

"On the edges of the lagoon in my native place", he says, "are bull-rushes and papyrus, 'like stars set in the trembling of the waves'; the marshy valleys full of water hyacinths (*Eichornia*), the broad, solemn plain, surrounded by mountains, is covered with different kinds of sunflowers, cosmos, tithonia and 'Spanish needles' (*Bidens*); while the 'Turkey's crest', *moco de guajolote* (*Polygonum pennsylvanicum*), spreads out in a carpet of bluish purple, the colour of the tapestries which hang from the altars in Holy Week; a huge carpet, smelling of clover, cassia and marjoram. In the rainy season, the *estrellitas*—white flowers with a deep yellow centre (*Galinsoga*?)—put a bridal veil over the hills; and away in the deep ravines, the tall yuccas are gay with clusters of ivory flowers; while on the plain the *Daturas* and *Ipomoeas* pour balm from their cups...."

"The simple flowers of my country adorn every phase of family life. The essential flower of the Indians is the *cempasuchil*, the Aztec marigold (*Tagetes erecta*), a violent yellow blossom with a strong, resinous scent. Baskets full of Aztec marigolds are watered by the Indians on November 2nd (All Souls' Day); bunches of marigolds are offered on the altars, and chains of marigolds cover the bosom of the bride on her wedding day. In the procession, bride and bridegroom are bound by garlands of marigolds; they wear enormous crowns of flowers, mirrors, pastry and silk ribbons of all colours—crowns more than a yard high, and so heavy that the wearers can hardly move their heads. A group of girls spreads petals of marigolds for the procession to pass."

With this natural love of flowers among a large part of the Indian and semi-Indian population, it is not surprising that the wild gardens, the natural gardens, should be more interesting than those more carefully cultivated. The park at Chapultepec and the trees and gardens which adorn the squares in many Mexican towns, are a proof of Mexican civilization; but the formal beds and imported trees are less memorable than the wilder plots, which have been preserved more or less in their original state, like Colonel Brocklebank's huge wild, wooded garden at San Antonio, Texas, which has now become the property—and the pride—of that sympathetic and friendly municipality.

"But is Mexico really so like Spain?" people ask me. An acute and observant Frenchman has described it as a Spanish landscape with Indian figures. But that will not do; the more you look at the landscape, and more especially at the vegetation, the less Spanish it seems; while the figures, which at first seem to give you all stages between pure Spaniards and pure Indians, are neither the one nor the other but a new race. It is a race still in process of formation; but it is being slowly welded together, and whatever it becomes eventually, it will not be European but American.

It was interesting to see how the so-called Spanish character of Mexico struck the Spanish Pilgrim Fathers who arrived on the *Sinaia*. They certainly had a friendly welcome. There certainly were cordial smiles from every passer-by. So far as understanding people from smiles went, the Spanish Pilgrims were in a good position to judge; for their journey had been made under eyes that were more inquisitive than sympathetic. Those frank smiles, coming after so much platform rhetoric and official handshaking, were proof of a real welcome. Yet in the midst of so much sympathy, and so many little attentions, there was always a faint suspicion of anxiety: "Do you find it like Spain?"

It was difficult (they said) to answer straight away. There was certainly a superficial resemblance to Spain: in the way people stood about in the streets, talking and laughing; in the voices, the street noises, blaring loud-speakers and ceaseless klaxons; shoeblacks, lottery tickets, people perpetually trying to sell you something; street markets, stalls on the pavement (as in parts of London, of course); iron *rejas* over the windows —all this was unmistakably Spanish. Spanish, too, was the manner of expression; a certain rather naïve way of feeling and reacting to the emotions; a taste for saying bitter things and eating peppery food. But did that mean that Mexico was really a Spanish country?

My Spanish friends doubt it, and my Mexican friends doubt it too. "The *conquistadores*", they say, "conquered Mexico because it was their duty. But, as with the conquests of Don Juan, they cared little what had happened before and even less what was likely to happen afterwards; they took what they could get, and did not trouble about the rest, which, in this case, was the most important part." There may be, here and there, an outline, an accent, a gesture, full of Spanish local colour: the skyline of the buildings, colours "which hit you like the bang of a daylight firework"; but there are two other characteristics as well: the ubiquitous signs of North American progress, and everywhere, in the background, the Indian. Spain, it is often said, is a blend of two traditions: the Visigothic and the Moorish (to say nothing of traces of Phoenician, Celtic and Roman). Mexico is a blend of three ingredients—Indian, Spanish and North American; but the most important for the future is the Indian.

Mexico is like Spain (and yet, unlike Spain) in much the same way as the United States—the Eastern United States— are like (and yet unlike) England. Is it a fundamental difference or a fundamental likeness? I should not like to say; some people may feel it one way, some another. But a short time after leaving the Mexican border, there is no doubt that you are in a country of people whose tradition is not Spanish, but English. This may seem a superficial impression, derived from a general "tarnish of achievement" which is not Spanish, and also from a certain sense of freedom and untidiness which are very Anglo-Saxon. It is difficult to say on what one's impressions rest; but after twenty years' experience—and procrastination—in Spanish-speaking countries, I feel that if I were dropped from an aeroplane in a parachute, I should know whether the country were Spanish before I had heard a word of the language.

I know now what the Spanish exiles must have felt on arriving at Veracruz; for I experienced it myself, crossing the Mexican Border into the United States at the beginning of the present war, and travelling slowly north-east, by San Antonio, New Orleans, Charleston, Williamsburg, Richmond—through Texas, Louisiana, Georgia, South Carolina, and Virginia—up to New York. Real sympathy for an individual Englishman, and for the whole English people; a certain distrust of what seemed to them the tortuous policy of the British Government and its somewhat distant and condescending attitude towards the United States (in spite of those war debts), combined with a very real anxiety for what might happen to England in the present emergency.

There was one other thing which I shall never forget, though it has probably happened to others beside myself. In the course of a good many journeys, and the crossing of a good many frontiers, I have had a good deal to do with immigration officials; but I never experienced anything to compare with the U.S. Inspector on the Mexican Border, when the formalities had been completed, and at a temperature officially registered as 99° in the shade: "Mr Trend, very pleased to have you pass through!"

INDEX

Ingram Content Group UK Ltd.
Milton Keynes UK
UKHW010851270623
424039UK00010B/132

9 781107 502055